Praise for *L*

In her new book, *Letting God Be Enough*, Erica Wiggenhorn speaks right to my heart. Like many women, I have struggled with feelings of inadequacy, fearful that I will never be enough. And while it is true that I will never be enough, I belong to a God who abundantly provides everything I need and more to fulfill His exciting purposes for me. From the story of Moses, Erica shows us how to trade our striving for surrender and replace our self-doubt with faith in the God who is more than enough. Solidly grounded in Scripture, *Letting God Be Enough* is a must-read for every woman who wonders if she is enough.

KATHY HOWARD | Bible teacher and author of ten books, including *Deep Rooted* and *Heirloom: Living and Leaving a Legacy of Faith*

*Letting God Be Enough* brings readers into the presence of Moses, where they discover a relatable guide wielding profound insights to light our journey of faith. Erica Wiggenhorn draws us a map out of insecurity and fear by inviting sojourners to venture deep into personal exploration. Her genuineness welcomes participants to pave this difficult path of Christ-centered confidence together. This Bible study resonates with my passion as a life coach and licensed therapist to fortify insecure minds, hearts, and souls to become heroes of their divine stories. I cannot recommend *Letting God Be Enough* highly enough.

TINA YEAGER | LMHC, award-winning author, speaker, *Flourish-Meant* podcast host, life coach

Do you struggle with inadequacy, fear, failure, or disappointment? Then *Letting God Be Enough* is the perfect book for you. Erica addresses the emotions we all feel—emotions that tell us we're not good enough. As she takes us on a journey through the life of Moses, we can relate to his struggles. And just as God proved Himself to be enough for

Moses, we can be confident that God is enough for us, no matter how overwhelming the situation may seem. You will be encouraged and spurred on in your own journey of faith. I needed this book!

CRICKETT KEETH | Author of *On Bended Knee: Praying like Prophets, Warriors, and Kings*; Women's Ministry Director at First Evangelical Church in Memphis, TN

Bestselling and award-winning author Erica Wiggenhorn is never afraid to tackle the tough topics in the Bible—and surrender is no exception. Through honest personal examples and stories, Erica exposes the deep inadequacies that lie deep within every heart. She answers questions like "What if I am not enough?" and "What if people don't like me?" with gut-wrenching vulnerability. But she doesn't leave us there. She not only combats the enemy's lies with the truth of in-depth study of Scripture, she leads us into a new promised land—one that begs us to leave behind the fears of yesterday and helps us forge ahead into a new tomorrow of an identity secure in Christ.

MICHELLE S. LAZUREK | Multi-genre award-winning author

Enough is a complicated word. A word I hear repeatedly in my counseling office. I'm done. I've had enough! Typically, my response is, "What are you done with? What do you mean by enough here?" With spiritual urgency, author Erica Wiggenhorn is saying, "I've had enough!" Enough of feeling inadequate. Enough of self-deprecating behavior and belief systems. Enough of jealousy and limiting mindsets. Enough of distraction and disappointment. In *Letting God Be Enough*, Erica becomes our well-versed and experienced trek leader and leads us into the terrain of Moses' life to show us God's processes and promises to bring Moses into new places of freedom. She's gone before us to get the lay of the land, to scout the flora and fauna, and serves as "a tent kicker" as we move through this adventure to our very own promised land of freedom.

JANELL M. RARDON | Author of *Stronger Every Day* and *Overcoming Hurtful Words*; trauma-informed therapist; founder, The Heartlift Practice

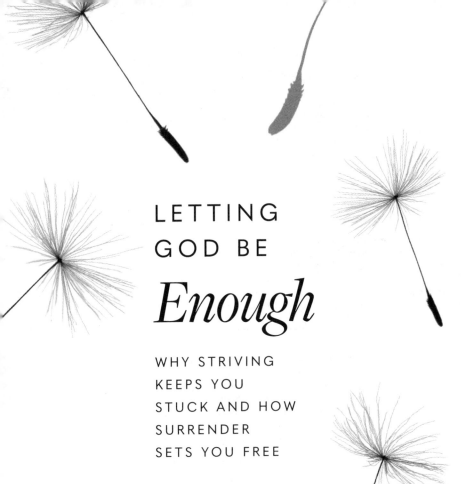

# LETTING GOD BE

## *Enough*

### WHY STRIVING KEEPS YOU STUCK AND HOW SURRENDER SETS YOU FREE

ERICA WIGGENHORN

**MOODY PUBLISHERS**

CHICAGO

Some content in chapter 1 is adapted from the author's book *Moses: Every Life Proof of God's Promises* (Bloomington, IN: CrossBooks, 2013).

Some content in chapter 12 is adapted from a blog post at ericawiggenhorn.com.

Scripture quotations are from the ESV® Bible (The Holy Bible, English Standard Version®), copyright © 2001 by Crossway, a publishing ministry of Good News Publishers. Used by permission. All rights reserved.

Published in association with The Steve Laube Agency.

Emphasis to Scriptures has been added by the author.

Some names and details of personal stories have been changed to protect privacy.

Edited by Pamela Joy Pugh
Interior design: Kaylee Lockenour
Cover design: Lauren Smith
Cover illustration of dandelion seeds copyright © 2009 by iSci / iStock (121915373). All rights reserved.
Author photo credit: Sarah Hoag Photography

Library of Congress Cataloging-in-Publication Data

Names: Wiggenhorn, Erica, author.
Title: Letting God be enough : why striving keeps you stuck and how
   surrender sets you free / Erica Wiggenhorn.
Description: Chicago, IL : Moody Publishers, [2021] | Includes
   bibliographical references. | Summary: "No matter how good we look
   externally, self-doubt is hard to shake. Erica Wiggenhorn draws from the
   story of Moses-the greatest self-doubter in the Bible-to show how
   self-doubt is tied closely to self-reliance. Only by casting yourself on
   God do you find the true source of strength"-- Provided by publisher.
Identifiers: LCCN 2021017791 (print) | LCCN 2021017792 (ebook) | ISBN
   9780802423313 | ISBN 9780802499639 (ebook)
Subjects: LCSH: Trust in God--Christianity. | Submissiveness--Religious
   aspects--Christianity. | Self-reliance. | Self-doubt. | Moses (Biblical
   leader) | BISAC: RELIGION / Christian Living / General | RELIGION /
   Christian Living / Calling & Vocation
Classification: LCC BV4637 .W486 2021  (print) | LCC BV4637  (ebook) | DDC
   248.4--dc23
LC record available at https://lccn.loc.gov/2021017791
LC ebook record available at https://lccn.loc.gov/2021017792

Originally delivered by fleets of horse-drawn wagons, the affordable paperbacks from D. L. Moody's publishing house resourced the church and served everyday people. Now, after more than 125 years of publishing and ministry, Moody Publishers' mission remains the same— even if our delivery systems have changed a bit. For more information on other books (and resources) created from a biblical perspective, go to www.moodypublishers.com or write to:

Moody Publishers
820 N. LaSalle Boulevard
Chicago, IL 60610

1 3 5 7 9 10 8 6 4 2

*Printed in the United States of America*

DEDICATED TO:

JESUS

*You are more than enough.*
*Thank You for taking me on this journey of freedom with You!*
*I pray that I have represented You well in these words.*

# CONTENTS

# A Moment of Decision to Pursue the Promised Land

My first real job. I was over the moon with excitement to work at my favorite clothing store in the mall, one I knew inside and out. As a high school girl, helping my friends put together outfits ranked as one of my top three favorite weekend activities. I was totally going to rock this!

Six weeks into the job, my manager asked me to help her start merchandising, which put me in charge of the display windows. I created the first impression everybody saw when they walked by the store while strolling through the mall. To say I loved my job was an understatement. I was giddy every time the delivery guy brought in a new shipment of clothes.

At the end of three months, my manager pulled me aside and informed me she had to do a performance review. "It's a standard thing. Don't worry. You're doing a great job!" Despite her encouraging words, I agonized over what she was going to say. Was I going to get fired? Did she hate how I arranged the window displays? I was certain she was going to let me go.

My fear of inadequacy enveloped me as I stared at the cute jackets on the mannequins. I wasn't catching my managers' vision. They didn't think my style arrangements attracted their target market and the sales dipped. Who did I think I was to be able to arrange store windows? What did I know about fashion anyway? The voices of impostor syndrome pounded in my head as the upbeat music echoed through the store. The longer I listened to those voices the further I spiraled down.

The day came for the review. We walked down to Chick-fil-A, but I could barely stomach my sandwich. I chewed nervously on my straw hopelessly trying to feign confidence as she pulled the review paper out of her purse. My worst fear was that my performance disappointed her, followed closely by a second one: she would hear my stifled shrieks of insecurity buried beneath my upbeat banter. This was the moment the real me would be exposed. All my creativity up to this point was merely a fluke. I was no fashion guru or marketing genius. I was a fraud, an impostor, who just happened to strike a few good poses in the window.

She held out the review sheet headed with the company logo and I just knew she was going to tell me how I wasn't measuring up. But she smiled. "Let's start with the great news: You're getting a raise and I'd like to promote you to assistant manager!"

I gulped and forced out, "Wow! Thank you!" I sat there stunned. I had been so certain she was going to publicly announce my deepest fear over Chick-fil-A sandwiches: *You're doing a good job, Erica, just not good enough.* I guess I wasn't going to get fired after all.

"You've been such a great asset to the company and you are one of the hardest-working employees I've ever had. Your attitude is always upbeat and your excitement to come into work energizes the whole team." I smiled weakly. I typically struggled with compliments. My insecurity hissed, *Wow, you've really fooled her!*

"Part of the review also means I have to give you a goal to work on." Here it comes. This is where she's going to point out a flaw. Up till now she was just being nice, and now the truth of my inadequacy is going to come out. I felt my leg muscles tighten beneath my skirt and the tension well up in my gut.

"You talk too much."

I could have focused on the raise and a promotion after only three months. But no, I would only continue to agonize over the one negative comment, which overshadowed every good thing she said. *You talk too much.*

My deep fear of inadequacy erupted out of me with violent force. The flaw surfaced to the top and seeped over, melting and covering every positive attribute she pointed out.

I'd love to tell you I confidently swept those feelings aside, but who can sweep away molten lava? It burns and hardens, changing the landscape permanently, leaving the positive hidden beneath it with no visible evidence left of what once shown beneath. Digging out from under feels hopeless.

Stuffing that fear of inadequacy creates an unstable and unpredictable environment—one that will explode in just the right set of circumstances leaving us shaking and out of control. I'd love to say I left behind that insecure teenager in the bright red booth at Chick-fil-A that Tuesday morning, but I'd be lying. She has followed me around for years, still nervous and fidgety, waiting to be told where she's falling short.

She still occasionally slides up next to me unexpectedly. Walking into a crowded room full of strangers. Starting a new job. Saying yes to something because I felt too insecure in the relationship to say no, yet simultaneously doubting I'd be able to meet their expectations anyway.

My ultimate moment of eruption occurred on my first visit to Moody Publishers. My first Bible study, *An Unexplainable Life*, had just released and I flew to Chicago to meet the team. My dear friend Kim, also an author at Moody, came too. Shortly before heading out to catch our cab, I began sweating and my hands began to shake. I whispered to her, "I can't do this. I can't go. I'm going to show up there, they are going to take one look at me and know they made a mistake publishing my study. Tell them I got sick!"

My no-nonsense friend looked me up and down and emphatically announced, "You have impostor syndrome! Google it right now!"

Kim doesn't take no for an answer, so I shakily pulled my phone out of my coat pocket. I typed "impostor syndrome" in the search bar and expected my own photo to pop up. Okay, not really. But the description of the thoughts, emotions, and lies I believed matched distinctly.[1] She whisked the phone out of my hand, guided me toward the door, and commanded, "We're going to put an end to this lie of the enemy right now. Out you go! We are going to Moody Publishers today and the team is going to adore you as much as I do. March, lady!" And we went.

I made it through the day. They didn't cancel my next contract and nobody on the team hated me. As I lay down that night I realized how I had allowed a complete lie to ruin a marked moment in my life. I got to visit Moody Publishers and see a book with my name on its cover on their shelves! And the whole time there I felt sick inside. I handed a moment of celebration over to the enemy to ruin because I believed his lies about God and about myself. God was enough to give me whatever I needed to write. And instead of rejoicing in a momentous occasion, I cowered in fear of inadequacy.

That fear of not having what it takes boils within, robbing us of the joy of any success we experience. It paralyzes us with fear that any shift in circumstances will swallow us with an inability to stand the quake. That inner nagging rumbles, taunting us with:

Am I enough?

If people really knew how I felt about myself, would they still accept me?

Will I be rejected when I can't perform?

Do I have what it takes to withstand this new season, circumstance, or assignment?

Can I pull this off?

What if I fail?

What if I end up alone?

Is this really all God has for me?

Am I missing out on the life I was meant to live because I can't shake this fear?

These questions flood our thoughts and drown out our ability to think clearly.

But what if, like a volcano, that process of eruption releases just enough tension to create a new balance? What if the minerals released in the explosion create a new landscape lush with fresh life? What if there was a way to remove the pent-up fear, to release crippling worry about unexpected and damaging activity erupting from within us, creating an irreversible landscape of "what ifs" and "if onlys"? What if someone could point out a path to navigate that barren landscape of nagging self-doubt and direct us to the promised land of abundant life?

> IT WAS TIME TO PUT AN END TO THIS LIE OF THE ENEMY. GOD IS ENOUGH TO FILL IN OUR GAPS. WE DON'T HAVE TO LOOK IN THE MIRROR AND FEEL LIKE WE HAVE EVERYTHING IT TAKES.

What if we could cease striving and surrender our endless cycles of frenetic performance?

Scripture offers us a life to examine: Moses. A monumental biblical figure. You might be familiar with his story. Born of Hebrew parents when Hebrews were slaves of the Egyptians. Hidden by his parents to escape the order for newborn Hebrew males to be put to death. Sent down the Nile to be pulled out of the water by no less than the Pharaoh's daughter. Raised in privilege, educated in the ways of a great civilization, yet aware of his heritage. As an adult, saw a Hebrew mistreated by an Egyptian and, enraged, kills the Egyptian, incurring the wrath of Pharaoh. So he runs away. He chooses to stay away from Egypt, the land of his upbringing, and seems to be content with a life of obscurity, tending sheep. But God doesn't allow him to stay there. He appears to Moses—you've heard of the burning bush—and begins to speak to him about His plans.

God uses words like:

Deliverance
Purpose and fulfillment
Relationship
Promised land

All the things Moses' life lacked because he remained bound in fear. God was going to release him from his desolation of self-doubt. The story of Moses' life in Scripture shows us God's processes and promises to bring Moses into new places of freedom—the promised land.

God guarantees that those same promises are available to us. The process requires some intentional trekking, but God guides us through every step, taking us past the desert of self-doubt into a new landscape flourishing with life. There may be some emotional eruptions along the way, but the place of promise proves worth the work. Because at the end of the journey, we find freedom, fulfillment, healthy human engagement, and the life we were created for.

So, lace up your hiking boots, friend. God is holding out His hand. If you're willing to grasp it, I'll grab your other one. We'll go together. Because neither one of us belongs stuck in the red booth at Chick-fil-A, forever paralyzed by our fear of inadequacy. That night in Chicago after my visit to Moody Publishers, I knew my friend Kim was right. It was time to put an end to this lie of the enemy. God is enough to fill in our gaps. We don't have to look in the mirror and feel like we have everything it takes. But we definitely aren't supposed to see ourselves as the poster child of impostor syndrome either. Instead, we are invited to believe God will always be enough whenever and however we fall short. And to stand tall in the promises He provides to us. There's a whole world of freedom, purpose, significance, and authentic relationships out there waiting for us—our promised land.

As we walk through the desert with Moses, we'll see what God can do with his sense of inadequacy—and ours. We'll talk about squashing fear, conquering jealousy, dealing with betrayal, and more, and even the need to have a "tent kicker" in our corner. Most of all, we'll talk about God Himself, and how He is trustworthy for us to let Him be enough.

At the close of each chapter, you'll find these features:

**Intentional Trekking** is a section of the following four components that invite you to pause and ponder the truths found in Scripture as you make connections between Moses' journey and your own personal steps from fear of inadequacy to freedom in letting God be enough.

**1. Bible Reading Plan:** This will put the story of Moses within scriptural context and connect you with God through His powerful, life-giving Word.

**2. Truths for the Journey:** Since all fears are rooted in lies, as we expose our false beliefs and thinking, we need to fill those spaces in our heart and mind with truth. These simple statements will help cement those truths about God and yourself within your mind, crowding out any space in which long-held lies about your worth have lived.

**3. Processing the Journey:** Last, we all need time to process our own journey with God. This is best done in the context of community, such as a book club, small group, Sunday school class, or online platform, but you can also use these questions for your own personal reflection and dialogue with God.

**4. Passionate Prayer:** This invites you to recite scriptural truths over your life, confessing areas where you are struggling to believe that God is able to silence those nagging voices of self-doubt and destructive feelings of inadequacy. You also are encouraged to ask God to reveal and remind you when He demonstrated the same aspects of His character to you throughout the course of your life. Let's get started now!

# Intentional Trekking

## Bible Reading Plan:
Exodus 1; Acts 7:17–38

## Truths for the Journey

- God doesn't allow us to stay in our desolation. He leads us out into new places.

- Scripture points out a path to navigate the barren landscape of nagging self-doubt and directs us to the promised land of abundant life.

- God promises to guide us through every step, taking us to our promised land.

- The place of promise proves worth the effort.

## Processing the Journey

1.  When and where have you had to receive constructive instruction or growth goals? How do you respond to others giving ideas for improvement?

2.  Which inner nagging question resonated with you most deeply? Why do you think this is so?

## Passionate Prayer

*Jesus, help me hear Your voice above all others. Help me believe what You say about me. Help me follow You fully to the places You have planned for me.*

## CHAPTER ONE

# Forging Our Identity

*But Moses said to God, "Who am I? . . ."*

*Exodus 3:11*

When I visit someone's home, I love to walk through their family rooms and hallways and look at their pictures. The snapshots that are displayed are usually the moments when the family is captured at their best. I often wonder where they were when the picture was taken and what they were doing. What were they thinking and feeling?

We recently had family photographs taken with my husband's entire side of the family at a beautiful Arizona resort. It took hundreds of attempts to capture just one single shot when all of us were looking at the camera with at least a somewhat normal expression on our face. Aged four to seventy-four, we came with quite diverse abilities to understanding the purpose of the perfect image.

When my mother-in-law proudly posted some of her favorites on Facebook, many people applauded her beautiful and happy family. We laughed at the comments, thinking of all it took to encapsulate the blissful scene!

While those photos are a wonderful memorial of what our family looked like that year, it is such a small picture of who we actually are. The background of the immaculately landscaped resort is a far cry from the dishes-piled, cluttered kitchen where I spend most of my days. The carefully matching clothes, neatly pressed and all tucked in do not reflect the frumpiness I feel when I slip on my old jeans that seem to get a little tighter every time I don them!

And the wide grins plastered across our faces? They don't give you an inkling of the arguments that went on as we combed our hair and put on our shoes. The worry that floods our minds when our heads hit the pillow at night didn't make it into the photo. Or the things we long to say to one another and just can't seem to find the right time or the right words. It's a snapshot.

> MOSES DOESN'T KNOW WHERE HE FITS AND WONDERS WHERE HE BELONGS. *MAYBE YOU CAN RELATE.*

There is so much more behind the scenes when we aren't standing still, looking our best, and posing for the camera. Emotions, hopes, dreams, and scars. Expectations, desires, and disappointments. While we all stand in the photo individually next to one another, the reality of a family is that we are all so intertwined, we often don't know where we ourselves end and our family begins.

Our family forges our identity. The definition of identity is "the fact of being who or what a person or thing is."[2]

Moses greatly struggled with his identity. Moses describes himself completely differently in Exodus 4 than the way Stephen does in Acts 7. You'd almost think they were talking about two different people! By piecing together bits of Moses' story, we gather the following about him:

He was physically attractive and others could see there was something unique about him (Ex. 2:2; Acts 7:20). The New International Version says "he was no ordinary child" (Heb. 11:23).

He was well-educated and a great speaker (Acts 7:22).

He grew up in the Egyptian royal household (Ex. 2:5–10), and was trained in all their ways (Acts 7:22), including the art of war.

Moses was a Hebrew being raised by an Egyptian princess. The Egyptians considered themselves culturally superior to the enslaved Hebrews (Ex. 8:25–27) but feared their growing numbers (Ex. 1:8–14). Yet Moses lived as an adopted Hebrew in Pharaoh's court. Despite the fact that he lived in luxury in the household of Pharaoh, he maintained a fascination toward his heritage and intentionally went out among the Hebrews to learn more about them.

As an adoptive mom, I understand this. While we are "Mom and Dad," our children are naturally curious about their biological ancestors. Moses wrestled between his Hebrew heritage and Egyptian nurturing. When identity is not clear during childhood, it can easily translate to a fear of inadequacy in adulthood. Our family helps define our place, our purpose, and a sense of meaning to our lives. If our family communicated that we were an accident, unwanted, an extra mouth to feed, a nuisance, or unlovable, those labels become written on our minds and flash the feelings of "not good enough" across our hearts with every beat.

At the age of forty, Moses ventured out among the Hebrew slaves, witnessed their oppression by the Egyptians and, in a rash moment, murdered an Egyptian overseer. When he returns among the Hebrew slaves the next day he asks them, "Why are you fighting with your fellow Hebrew?" Frankly, Moses' question seems a bit naïve, as though the Hebrews were one big, happy family who never quarreled.

Let's imagine what may have gone through the mind of the Hebrew slave. "Well, let's see, Moses, I could answer your question in so many ways. I'll start by reminding you that we're both oppressed slaves. We spend most of our waking hours toiling under the burning Egyptian sun performing excessive manual labor. We both are frequently mocked and abused by our Egyptian overseers as you yourself witnessed yesterday. But yes, I get your point, we should be kind and loving toward one another, because we are both Hebrews."

Maybe that's why he answers Moses with such sarcasm and disdain saying, "Who made you judge and ruler over us?" which in actuality, as the prince of Egypt, is exactly who Moses was! His answer basically informs Moses, "You obviously have not a clue what it means to be a Hebrew!"

A piece of Moses emotionally identifies with his Hebrew brothers, but they reject him. And deep down he knows he is not, or will ever be, a true Egyptian. He lacks identity. He doesn't know where he fits and wonders where he belongs. Moses sought to forge his own identity by becoming the deliverer of the Hebrew people. But his Operation Deliverance backfired. They neither recognized him as their deliverer nor accepted him as their brother. Moreover, Pharaoh's anger at Moses for committing the murder of an Egyptian forced him to flee to Midian. Moses faced rejection from everyone to whom he looked for his identity. And his failure to deliver the Israelites became his proof that he indeed was inadequate.

Maybe you can relate. The people who were supposed to encourage you laughed at your dreams. You sensed a call of God on your life, a stirring passion to follow God in a certain area or role. Just one strike spoken over you and you counted yourself out. Been there, done that.

Maybe it was a teacher who didn't like your writing.

Maybe it was a coach who always insisted you kept doing things wrong.

Maybe it was a pragmatic parent who told you to put your energy toward a "real" career.

Maybe it was a sibling or friend who seemed to be amazing while you remained only adequate.

Maybe it was a boss you could never satisfy, or a spouse you were unable to make happy.

Maybe it's a child struggling in school or life.

Somewhere along the way the message got through: *I just don't have what it takes.*

But Moses is about to discover the secret to identity, to uncover the fact of being who, or what, a person is. He asks God for the answer. Who am I, God? This is the first step. Even our family members don't know us to the core. Sure, they get more than a snapshot, but there are thoughts, dreams, and emotions within us we may never have expressed to them. We have gifts and abilities they never took the time to unwrap, display, or foster. They never bothered to gaze intently inside of us and discover all that we are.

God, however, knows everything about us as we are shown in Psalm 139:1–4.

> *O LORD, you have searched me and known me!*
>
> *You know when I sit down and when I rise up;*
>
> *you discern my thoughts from afar.*
>
> *You search out my path and my lying down*
>
> *and are acquainted with all my ways.*
>
> *Even before a word is on my tongue,*
>
> *behold, O LORD, you know it altogether.*

God knows every fact about you. In fact, He uniquely created you just as you are on purpose.

> *For you formed my inward parts;*
>
> *you knitted me together in my mother's womb.*
>
> *I praise you, for I am fearfully and wonderfully made. (vv. 13–14)*

And God calls what He created good, better than good!

> *Wonderful are your works;*
>
> *my soul knows it very well. (v. 14b)*

And made for great purpose.

*In your book were written, every one of them,*
*the days that were formed for me. (v. 16)*

God knows you—the real you. He is the only one who can fully forge your identity, because He is the only one who knows you deeply enough to be able to do so . . . even more deeply than you know yourself. So, while your family—biological or otherwise— may have communicated that you're not enough, that your dreams are unattainable or your existence insignificant, the God who created you says otherwise. And while the family in which you were raised may have felt less than ideal or even destructive, God placed you there for a purpose.

As long as we insist that we need to be accepted by people before we can fulfill our purpose, our fear of not being enough will isolate us. No human connection can provide the ultimate validation we crave—only I AM will be enough to fulfill us.

For Moses to accomplish all that God had planned for him, life in Pharaoh's palace proved the perfect training ground for him. He would've been taught how to read and write to record the Law that would later be entrusted to him, how to conduct battle to fight the enemies of Israel, mathematics and architecture to construct the tabernacle and its furnishings, and government to organize the over two million people that he would need to lead and oversee. Little did he know as he was being raised and educated how all that information would be used, but God was planting seeds of knowledge that would blossom at His perfect time for His purposes.

ONLY GOD CAN REWRITE THE REVERBERATING FEARS OF THE PAST INTO SONGS OF SECURITY IN THE FUTURE.

Moses' upbringing in Pharaoh's court may not have provided solid emotional attachment to his Egyptian mother. He may have longed for acceptance from his Hebrew brothers. But God promised to provide for Moses the connection and identity he so desperately sought, yet failed to receive, from his fellow Israelites. It was Moses' painful experience of rejection that allowed him to marvel over being personally chosen by God.

I would dare bet that, like Moses, some of your familial relationships are messy, confusing, frustrating, and disappointing. Sometimes they can even be heartbreaking or destructive. Moses experienced all those emotions through his human relationships and guess what? He learned to seek the Lord in the midst of the disappointment and devastation, and discovered that his relationship with the Lord was the only one that brought some wholeness to all the other broken ones. If not wholeness, well then, at least, acceptance.

> FOR MOSES TO ACCOMPLISH ALL THAT GOD HAD PLANNED FOR HIM, LIFE IN PHARAOH'S PALACE PROVED THE PERFECT TRAINING GROUND FOR HIM.

Friendship with I AM forged the path to answer the question, "But, who am I?" Coming to God with this question is the first step in the journey toward the promised land. Rather than continuing to read the flashing labels of "not good enough" and drowning in feelings of self-doubt, we turn to God for a new script. In order to fully embrace God's answer, we need to empty ourselves of the inadequate answers that have previously been spoken over us. Our fear of not being enough comes from a misplaced identity. We may understand pieces of ourselves, but we haven't allowed God to reveal to us all that we are.

Only God can rewrite the reverberating fears of the past into songs of security in the future. Belonging to Him, being His, places us into a new family, a new identity, with sacred callings and inestimable worth. He makes us enough—more than enough—and He thunders through His Word, teaching us to tune our ears toward His truth. And then our feelings begin to follow.

It's a process. Sometimes a longer one than we'd like. But God is faithful to keep speaking truth to us each and every time we turn to Him and ask, "But, who am I, God?" The transformation happens slowly, bit by bit, each time we draw near and allow the Master Composer to play a new song of truth over us. It's a dance just between the two of us—God and me. God and you.

At this point in Moses' life, he holds a lot of knowledge, but lacks wisdom. He continues playing the old tunes of his rejection from the Israelites and past failure in his head. God is going to have to get him alone with Him for a while in order to impart the truth of who He is and who Moses is. And God invites you, dear one, to step into His arms and begin this same dance—just the two of you—listening to His voice of truth and silencing that old script of self-doubt.

# Intentional Trekking

**Bible Reading Plan:**
Exodus 2; Psalm 139

## Truths for the Journey

- The definition of identity is "the fact of being who or what a person or thing is."
- The secret to discovering our identity is to ask God who we are.
- Even our family members don't know us to the core, but God knows everything about us.
- God is the only one able to fully forge your identity because He is the only one who knows you fully.
- It was Moses' painful experience of rejection that allowed him to marvel over being personally chosen by God.

## Processing the Journey

1. What is something that other people have said you are good at?

2. Who knows you better than anyone else? How did you develop that closeness?

3. Who in your family encouraged your dreams?

4. What are some things you learned growing up in your family that have been useful as an adult?

5. Why is God the only one who can truly help us understand the fact about who we are? Why can't others' perceptions of us be taken as facts?

## Passionate Prayer

*Dear Jesus, I confess that there are things I don't like about myself. I acknowledge that You made me the way You did on purpose and with a purpose. No one knows me more fully than You. Show me what it means to find my identity in and through You. Help me believe that what others have said are only perceptions. You alone know the facts about who I really am.*

## CHAPTER TWO

# *Forging Ahead After Failure*

*But he said to me, "My grace is sufficient for you,*
*for my power is made perfect in weakness." Therefore,*
*I will boast all the more gladly of my weaknesses,*
*so that the power of Christ may rest upon me.*

2 Corinthians 12:9

My dad used to jokingly say about my husband, "Jonathan will be successful at anything he does, or at least he'll die trying!" He meant that as a compliment regarding his perseverance, yet there are people who would almost rather die than fail at something. People tell us that sometimes failure is our greatest teacher, but if we took a poll, I'd wager that just about everybody would vote to receive instruction through another means. Moses ran ahead of God, taking matters into his own hands rather than waiting on His timing. Sometimes in our fear of inadequacy we can become so desperate to prove ourselves, we will rush ahead to tackle something just to prove our worth. Moses sensed the call to deliver his people from the Egyptians, but the plan failed. And Moses ran away to hide. What's interesting to me is where he chose to go. Moses fled into the wilderness, a place of total obscurity. Attempting to create a new identity, he denied his giftedness and valuable life experiences, and instead, performed one of the most debased jobs in ancient society—shepherding.

> WE HAVE TO ALLOW GOD TO FORGE OUR NEW IDENTITY OR WE'LL SETTLE FOR COMFORTABLE RATHER THAN CHASE THE MIRACULOUS.

Surely he could have gone to Ur or Shechem, or another large city and worked as an accountant or even a teacher. Instead he chose a life for the poor and uneducated. Moses is strong, articulate, and presumably trained in the best schools in Egypt. But he goes to no-man's-land doing a job people whose options were more limited than an educated member of the Egyptian royal household typically did. And Scripture tells us that Moses was content to stay there (Ex. 2:21). Initially Moses' fear of inadequacy pushed him into proving himself through an epic performance, but after his one-man Operation Deliverance failed he fled to passivity and obscurity.

This seems so strange to me, but if I'm honest with myself, I'd often rather choose something easy than risk failure. Sometimes in my life I've called this course of action *wise*. Other times I've called it *responsible*. I've even gone so far as to call it *noble* as life unfolded, and taking risks meant involving others dear to me such as my husband and children. And the reality is that God has not wasted any steps of that path. But if I am honest with myself, I recognize that I've taken on a lot of roles and activities in my life more to deflect my fear of inadequacy and try and prove my worth, than because I sensed God calling me to those roles at the time.

If we know the story of Moses' life, we can certainly see how forty years of shepherding served him well herding the people of Israel through the wilderness. God had purpose even in this path that didn't make any sense based on Moses' skill set.

Moses is about to begin adulting. He gets married and settles down. Starts a family. We still see his identity struggle. He names his son Gershom, which in Hebrew means "expulsion" or "resident alien there,"[3] for heaven's sake. Listen to what he says: "I have been a sojourner in a foreign land" (Ex. 2:22). He lives here, works here, his family is here, but what is Moses still feeling deep down? "I don't belong here. There's something else out there, somewhere else I should be."

Maybe you're near this stage of life. Maybe you've chosen the wise or responsible path in life. You forfeited a dream because it felt selfish to pursue it. Taking a steady job or staying home full time felt like a more noble endeavor. And truthfully, any sacrifice we make for the good of those we love should be viewed as such. But maybe you wrestle with the nagging feeling that there is something more for you: deeper, more meaningful relationships, the spouse you're hoping to find, a new career path or dream to pursue once the kids are more independent. There's something within you that stirs for something more. But you're living in Midian. And for now, you are content to dwell there, but inwardly you know you eventually belong somewhere else.

Something else significant is happening here also. Moses is passing his "I don't fit in anywhere" complex onto his son, reminding him by his name that he isn't really a Midianite either. We have to face our insecurities and allow God to forge our new identity or we'll pass down the shackles of self-doubt to the next generation. We'll live guarded rather than loving generously. We'll settle for comfortable rather than chase the miraculous. If we live fearing that failure waits around every corner because our script of self-doubt directs our steps, so will our children.

Moses believed he didn't belong anywhere—neither with the Egyptians nor the Israelites nor the Midianites. And you know what?

He was right. He would never be Egyptian. He was not intended to be a Hebrew slave. It was not his future to remain a Midianite shepherd. God's plan for Moses was for him to be different—set apart. He wasn't called to *be* one of the Israelites, he was called to *lead* the Israelites. He belonged to God. He was called out by God and equipped by God for a unique role and purpose within the history of the world.

And friend, you may not fully believe this yet, but *so are you.*

Moses' fear of inadequacy may have originated from the lack of belonging he felt in the Egyptian royal court and the rejection he faced from his Hebrew brothers. Or, it's from his disappointment in fulfilling the nudge he felt in his heart to help deliver them. But God, in His infinite wisdom, placed Moses in those situations to open his eyes to see with whom he actually belonged: God. Every disappointment and rejection drove him to the One who would forever fulfill and accept him as His own.

Let that sink in for a moment.

The disappointments you've endured, the rejection you've withstood, even the failures you faced . . . they may have led you to inward feelings of self-doubt, but God means them to serve as your road map to Christ. And it's He in whom all security and sufficiency are ultimately found.

Each one of us as followers of Jesus has been given a unique gift to be employed in good works for our time and place in history. Yet as long as Moses focused on his past failure and his need for acceptance by others, he would never embrace those truths. He would forever feel like a failure and doubt his ability to do what God asked of him. He would choose an easier path and other endeavors rather than the grand adventure God had for him. And friend, so will we if we don't get serious about understanding our identity and conquering our fear of inadequacy.

Yet even in this place of obscurity and waiting, God was equipping Moses. God knew what He was accomplishing in mundane Midian. Listen to this perspective:

"For 40 years . . . Moses undertook the toilsome life of a sheepherder in the Sinai area, thus gaining valuable knowledge of the topography of the Sinai Peninsula which later was helpful as he led the Israelites in that wilderness land."[4]

And further, "Egypt accomplished him as a scholar, a gentleman, a statesman, a soldier, all which accomplishments would be afterwards of use to him, but yet he lacked one thing, in which the court of Egypt could not befriend him. He that was to do all by divine revelation must know, by a long experience, what it was to live a life of communion with God; and in this he would be greatly furthered by the solitude and retirement of a shepherd's life in Midian."[5]

> THE DISAPPOINTMENTS YOU'VE ENDURED MAY HAVE LED YOU TO INWARD FEELINGS OF SELF-DOUBT, BUT GOD MEANS THEM TO SERVE AS YOUR ROAD MAP TO CHRIST.

And friend, can I remind you today, that God knows what He is accomplishing in this season of your life? You may yearn for more. You may feel like an alien in a foreign land, unique, isolated, or alone. The days may feel monotonous, insignificant, or meaningless. You may wonder where you fit and where you belong. But the story of Moses reminds us that God is at work.

Our early days in Arizona felt like Midian. We left the verdant leafy trees of North Carolina for a dirt backyard surrounded by brown mountains and tan houses. The scene outside my kitchen window felt as dull and colorless as my days. With a preschooler and a toddler, some days seemed to repeat in endless cycles with little evidence of any sort of progress or accomplishment. But this season also included daily naptimes, where I began to forge the habit of connecting with God in the silence . . . a habit I carried with me beyond Midian into even fuller seasons of life, when I didn't have little ones keeping me at home and quiet for two hours every afternoon.

Midian also provided an opportunity to establish friendships with other moms to survive the chaos of the remaining hours when my young children were awake! Those friendships proved integral throughout Midian but also beyond, as my children got older and God began to call me to new things. I need those friends as much today as I did in Midian.

Midian is the place where we learn to listen. Those haunting echoes of our inadequacy begin to be drowned out by the soothing sounds spoken over us by the Savior as we open His Word, allowing Him to place a new song within our ever-racing minds. Because often when we are in Midian we cannot see how God is working. We are surrounded by duties and our schedule feels too daily. Responsibilities weigh heavy and the horizon looks flat and desolate.

It's often in faithfully carrying out our responsibilities that God gifts us with meaningful relationships. And while Moses may feel alone in his identity, God was using the time to forge a friendship between Moses and Jethro, his father-in-law, that would have a great effect on his life. We'll see later how Jethro celebrated with Moses, redirected him when he got overwhelmed, and warned him when he began to make unhealthy choices. It was the dailyness and drudgery of Midian that the early bonds of trust between the two were formed.

Don't you find it marvelous how each stage and circumstance in Moses' life was so perfectly planned and designed to equip him for his unique call? Furthermore, don't you love how patient God is in preparing us for ours? What Moses still didn't yet know was that God's plan for his life was unfolding exactly the way God had intended. From Moses' limited perspective, he may have thought himself a failure, but from God's point of view, Moses was positioned exactly where God wanted him.

*And so are you.* Lean in and listen. Pieces of your past are preparation for the future God has planned for you. The winds of change begin to stir across your desert landscape as the voice of the Almighty speaks new truth about your identity.

# *Intentional Trekking*

## Bible Reading Plan:
Exodus 2; 2 Corinthians 12:9

## Truths for the Journey

- God has purpose in the path even when it doesn't make sense or seem to fit our skill set.
- Midian is the place where we learn to listen.
- It's often in faithfully carrying out our responsibilities that God gifts us with meaningful relationships.
- Pieces of your past are preparation for the future God has planned for you.

## Processing the Journey

1. Second Corinthians 12:9 follows the well-known phrase about Paul's "thorn in the flesh." What is God's answer? Describe in your own words what you think Paul is saying here. How does verse 9 outline the paradox of having power to overcome our fear of not being good enough?

2. Why do you think Moses chose to flee to Midian rather than capitalizing on his skills and education to find other means of employment?

3. Describe what a modern-day Midian season might look like. Have you ever been in Midian? Are you in Midian now?

4. Have you altered your dreams, fulfilled your dreams, or completely abandoned them? Was there a significant life event or encounter that prompted you to take that course of action?

5. Who has become a meaningful relationship in your life that was forged through faithfully fulfilling your responsibilities?

## Passionate Prayer

*Dear Jesus, teach me what faithfulness looks like in my Midian. Make me faithful in my daily responsibilities enjoying Your presence with me even in the most mundane tasks. Open my eyes to those You have placed around me to forge deep friendships. Open my heart to be willing to invest in them and invite them into my life. Help me not to compare my life to others, but to trust that You have me exactly where You want me for this season.*

## CHAPTER THREE

# The Real Rescuer

*"I have observed you and what has been done to you in Egypt, and
I promise that I will bring you up out of the affliction of Egypt . . ."*
*Exodus 3:16–17*

Watching my son play soccer ranks as one of my favorite
weekend activities. Now that he is a teenager, the games require much more skill and strategy than in years prior. His team
wins when they play wisely and employ skills possessed through
many hours of practice. Mama Bear gets pretty passionate on the
sidelines encouraging the team and I've been dubbed the Team
Cheerleader who rallies the other parents to chime in with me. We
often bellow, "You've got this, boys! You can do it! Don't give up!
You know what to do!"

This all sounds well and good and everyone needs encouragement,
but sometimes in life, we just "ain't got it." We face circumstances
and seasons where we know we are only going to be able to make it
through by the grace of God.

This is when the fear sets in, because we cannot rely on ourselves.
We are realistic about our inability to be enough in our current

situation. We look within ourselves and unequivocally know we just don't have the power to eradicate cancer, equip a loved one to overcome an addiction, put the prodigal on the path back home, or look into the future with certainty of the outcome we so desperately desire. We can't do it and we don't know what to do. We are inadequate.

God never asked Moses to consider himself or his abilities. God implored Moses in Exodus 3:14 to consider who *He* is: "I AM WHO I AM." God never tried to convince Moses that he had what it took to get the job done. He never reminded him how he had received the finest education in the ancient world. He didn't replay the scene when Moses single-handedly drove away a crowd of shepherds, coming to the rescue of Jethro's daughters. God never mentioned one single attribute of either Moses' skills, life experiences, or character.

*God simply asked Moses to believe Him.*

When we walk methodically through the dialogue between God and Moses in the burning bush encounter at Horeb, the mountain of God, we notice a couple of striking truths. God says the following things to Moses in Exodus 3:7–10:

"I have surely seen the affliction of my people."
"I have . . . heard their cry."
"I know their sufferings."
"I have come down to deliver them."
"[I will] bring them up . . . to a good and broad land."
"I will send you to Pharaoh that you may bring my people, the children of Israel, out of Egypt."

Take a look at that list. Who is doing all the work? Whose plan and power does God invoke? Moses is simply the messenger. Yet even in this, he wavers, asking God, "Why me?"

God doesn't really answer Moses' question. He doesn't remind Moses how he grew up in the Egyptian royal household learning both the culture and the language, so he can converse effectively with Pharaoh. He doesn't gesture with His almighty arm reminding Moses how he has pastured flocks all over the Sinai and knows the land inside and out to effectively lead the people on the quickest route to the promised land. He doesn't bring up Moses' past failures, reminding him how he had tried to deliver the people years ago by his own power and plan. He doesn't actually mention one thing about Moses' abilities at all. Instead, God offers Moses a promise: *I will be with you, and when it's all said and done, Moses, you'll end up right back here at Horeb, where you started. We'll make it all the way back home again, together.*

Why doesn't God affirm Moses' skills and background? For a guy who clearly struggles with identity and inadequacy, a few props from God would've been welcomed. But God doesn't give them to him. Instead He gives Moses the promise of Himself—His presence with Moses the whole way there and back. I think the significance of God's answer goes even deeper than just the comfort of His continual care. I think God knows Moses is really asking an even deeper question than "Why me?" Maybe what Moses really wanted to know sounded more like this:

*What if I'm too afraid?*
*What harm will come to me?*
*Will they recognize me as the chosen deliverer this time?*
*What if I blow it again?*
*Will I be able to cope if I face another failure?*

God answers the unspoken cries of Moses' heart, not the rash words he blurts out of his mouth. In God's simple answer of "I will be with you," God assures Moses of so many things.

*You won't be doing it alone this go-around, Moses.*
*You will make it out alive and return to this very place along with the people of Israel and worship Me here.*
*They will believe you and you will not fail.*

The One who knows our thoughts before they are uttered on our lips knows what Moses is wondering deep down within the caverns of his heart. The promises of God pierce into the inner cries of our soul giving voice and peace to our silent fears. And it is often when these fears are spoken we can process them effectively.

WHAT MOSES REALLY WANTS TO KNOW IS IF GOD CAN GUARANTEE THE OUTCOME HE HAS PROMISED OR NOT. WOULD GOD BE ENOUGH?

If I'm honest, though, I often do what Moses did. I don't ask God to reassure me regarding my deepest fears; instead, I bombard Him with superfluous questions, too afraid to address what I'm really feeling. And sometimes, even when God does answer the deep questions I'm too afraid to verbalize, I still swim in a sea of doubt and emotion looking for someone or something else to bring me to shore.

God's reply did not convince Moses, so he asks God some more questions. He asks God what His name is. "If ancient cultures considered something to exist when it had a name and a function, the name of a deity is more than simply a moniker by which he or she can be invoked. It is the god's identity and frames the god's 'existence.'"[6]

Moses is trying to get to the root of who God is and what function He serves. In the ancient world of polytheism, "gods" were much different than I AM, the God of Abraham, Jacob, and Isaac who was speaking to Moses. Each had a purpose, such as overseeing the weather or crops or fertility. Moses is essentially asking God, "Okay, what exactly is Your purpose, and how trustworthy are You in fulfilling it?" The Egyptian gods of Moses' time were not always reliable either in their actions or their character. What Moses really wants to know is if God can guarantee the outcome He has promised or not. Can he trust God to be enough?

When we face a situation in which we cannot secure the outcome, our loss of control makes us afraid. While we believe that God is all powerful and is able to deliver any outcome He so desires, we wrestle with whether or not He wills it. In other words, we believe God is able to *make good* on His promises, but we wonder if He is willing to *be good* on our behalf. Our definition of God being good usually equates to Him giving us what we really want. Is God's character truly good even when He doesn't give us the outcome we ask Him for?

God's answer to Moses' question addresses both His capability and His character. I AM WHO I AM (Ex. 3:14). This is the same as the Hebrew "LORD" that we see written so many times in the Old Testament. It is the name that the Hebrew people would not dare utter and wrote without vowels because they held such reverence for it. It is the covenant name with Abraham: Yahweh. It means "a God who creates" in the sense of "a God who enters a relationship."[7]

The Israelites had heard the name Yahweh before, but this function of relationship was one they had not yet experienced. It is in the context of a relationship that we become confident of one's character.

What is God explaining to Moses? "I am the God who creates a people for Myself for the purpose of having a relationship with them." He tells Moses that He is "the God of your fathers." Relationship. Remember, Moses does not identify with the Egyptians, is not accepted by the Hebrews, and does not consider himself a Midianite. He longs for relationship, to understand who he is and where he belongs. Suddenly, Moses' prospect of finally finding his identity burns through the flames of self-doubt: Yahweh has appeared, issuing His call on Moses' life.

God, the creator of relationship, is both capable and kind. He invites us into a place of intimacy where we can become confident

> WHEN GOD CALLS US TO A CIRCUMSTANCE OR SEASON OF LIFE THAT IS OUT OF OUR CONTROL, HE DOESN'T REMIND US OF ALL THE REASONS WE CAN RELY ON OURSELVES. INSTEAD, HE PROMISES HIS PRESENCE WILL GO WITH US AND WE'LL MAKE IT BACK HOME.

of His character . . . even when He secures an outcome we would not have chosen. He loves us too much to give us anything less than what is best. When God calls us to a circumstance or season of life that is out of our control, He doesn't remind us of all the reasons we can rely on ourselves. Instead, He promises His presence will go with us and we'll make it back home.

As we trek through Moses' journey toward the promised land of silencing self-doubt and those nagging feelings of a fear of not being good enough, we'll see Moses' fear of inadequacy envelop him. Each time, God tenderly meets Moses in his moment of angst. He speaks to the fear and promises His aid. Never once does God ask Moses to focus on his own introspection, skill set, or strength. Instead, God patiently and faithfully reveals a new aspect of Himself to Moses—calming his fears and lifting his gaze above the circumstances. As Moses' relationship with God grows, so does his confidence in God's character.

We will see God call Himself by new names, reminding Moses that He would always and forever be enough to deliver on His promises. This is the care of the great I AM. As we rest in our identity that we are chosen, called, and equipped by our loving heavenly Father, our own fear of inadequacy becomes enveloped within His mighty arms of grace. We will never be adequate within ourselves, but I AM will always be enough. He's got this.

# *Intentional Trekking*

## Bible Reading Plan:
Exodus 3

## Truths for the Journey

- We face circumstances and seasons where we know we are only going to be able to make it through by the grace of God.

- God never asked Moses to look at himself or at his abilities. God simply asked Moses to believe Him.

- God gives us the promise of Himself—His presence the whole way home.

- The promises of God pierce into the inner cries of our soul, giving voice and peace to our silent fears.

- We believe God is able to *make good* on His promises, but we wonder if He is willing to *be good* on our behalf.

- As Moses' relationship with God grows, so does his confidence in God's character. It is in the context of a relationship that we become confident of one's character.

## Processing the Journey

1. God never mentioned one single attribute of either Moses' skills, life experiences, or character. God simply asked Moses to believe Him. What is something about God you struggle to believe? Why do you think you struggle as you do?

2. Can you share a time when God revealed an aspect of Himself to you that calmed your fear?

3. Is it easier for you to believe in God, or in yourself? Why?

4. With which do you struggle more—believing in God's character, or in His capabilities?

5. Describe a time when you felt God's presence in your life. What is a situation or circumstance you are currently facing in which the promise of God's presence brings you great comfort?

6. What are some practical ways we can become more confident of God's character?

7. What does it mean to you that God chose to address Moses as the God who enters into relationship with His people? What do you think it would have meant to Moses?

## Passionate Prayer

*Dear Jesus, help me believe You. In the greatness of
Your capabilities and the goodness of Your character.
Forgive me when I view You as less than all that You are.
Help me remember that Your presence is always with me and
You will never leave me. Help me pursue a deeper relationship
with You in Your Word and through prayer that I may grow
more confident of both Your character and Your capabilities.*

## CHAPTER FOUR

# God's Game Plan

*" . . . that they may believe that the LORD, the God*
*of their fathers, the God of Abraham, the God of Isaac,*
*and the God of Jacob, has appeared to you."*

*Exodus 4:5*

My printer died last week. Spit out its last piece of paper and went kaput. After a mad dash to Costco to get a new one, I came home to attempt the installation. The last time I bought a printer it came with a disc to insert into my laptop that magically told my computer what to do. My current laptop no longer had a disc drive and my new printer didn't come with an installation disc. Instead it came with a URL to download a 97–page pdf with step-by-step directions on how to link my new printer to my computer. I turned the computer off and waited for my husband to come home. I was not even going to try.

Installing a printer hardly changes the landscape of our life in drastic ways. But I've taken this approach in other areas of my life also. When I thought I knew how to do something but then the game changed, I chucked the playbook and gave up. I did not want to do it

LETTING GOD BE ENOUGH

a new way. But our God is in the business of doing new things, which also means He does things in new ways.

And what was God's plan in Exodus 3? It was time for the enslaved Hebrews to leave Egypt. And who would lead them? Moses was not enthusiastic about God's choice, which felt to him as user-friendly as navigating a 97-page downloadable pdf. Sometimes having the instructions isn't enough. We need further assurance to overcome our fear of inadequacy. I love what God does for Moses in this moment.

God takes this exhaustive chronology of instructions and summarizes it for Moses. Look closely at God's game plan in Exodus 3:17–21:

"I promise . . ."

"I will bring you up . . ."

"I know that the king of Egypt will not let you go . . ."

"I will stretch out my hand . . ."

"I will give this people favor . . ."

Essentially, God becomes that magical installasion disc who does all the work. Moses just has to install it. He doesn't have to pull up the pdf and read step one, two, three, three hundred. When we wrestle with deep fears of inadequacy, knowing how to do something does not necessarily prove all that comforting. We still wonder if we are able to pull it off. Maybe the knowledge exists, but the skill set to take the knowledge and apply it remains questionable. Or we undeniably assert our inability to accomplish it, regardless of knowing the action plan.

Sometimes we just turn off the computer and walk away without even making an attempt. Other times we defer to other people. Moses tried to do both.

Then Moses answered, "But behold, they will not believe me or listen to my voice, for they will say, 'The LORD did not appear to you.'" (Ex. 4:1)

The pdf isn't enough, Lord, I need something or someone else.

But Moses said to the LORD, "Oh, my Lord, I am not eloquent, either in the past or since you have spoken to your servant, but I am slow of speech and of tongue."—Exodus 4:10

There you have it. Even with a pdf, I cannot cut it.

By the way, you might notice two different renderings of the word "Lord" in this verse. The spelling LORD is the way Yahweh is spelled in English translations of the Hebrew. The Hebrew "Lord" is a reference to God that means He is the master. Moses objects to the Master's plan. Let that sink in. In Moses' eyes, God's character and His capabilities have become questionable and fear reigns in his heart now. Our inability to trust and obey God reflects our lack of intimacy with His character and imperception of His limitless power. "Moses knew of God as a distant Sovereign but not as the immanent God who cares for and loves His chosen ones."[8] Moses wondered exactly how vested God would remain in the deliverance operation along with how capable He was in pulling it off.

> GOD CREATED YOU TO ENTER INTO RELATIONSHIP WITH YOU. HE KNOWS EVERY SINGLE ONE OF YOUR CAPABILITIES AND YOUR GIFTING.

In ancient Near Eastern cultures like Egypt, people believed in a pantheon of gods. Not all gods were equal. They could outsmart and trick one another. They were also fickle and self-serving. People held much different views of deity than we do in our twenty-first century Western world, where most of us have had some access to the Bible and at least a rudimentary explanation of the Christian God. Many of us were even raised singing, "Jesus loves me, this I know." Some of us have been able to go deeper than the basics. If we are honest, however, we still can wrestle with wondering if and how God might come through for us.

Moses knows that even with a game plan, he himself cannot guarantee a win. There are still too many variables he cannot control. The people might reject him. He lacks communication skills. In

Moses' mind he just does not have what it takes. But Moses also implies something else by raising objections. He questions whether God's really got this. Sure, God sounds like He has a good plan, but can He actually deliver a win?

Or maybe a deeper question: How capable am I of messing up God's plan? If God sends me—and I actually make an attempt at Operation Deliverance—when I mess up, will the whole plan fail? I mean, who wants to be the human who thwarts divine plans?

This is where God's name "LORD" becomes so profound. As we've seen, LORD, Yahweh, means the "God who creates" or the "God who enters relationship." God created you to enter into relationship with you. He knows every single one of your capabilities and your gifting. He also knows when you can't install a printer. He *gets* you. He did not create you to become dependent on you. He created you to be dependent on Him—to find in a relationship with Him life's fullest meaning.

Moses needs something and someone else. Moses does not realize it yet, but the "somes" are God. He needs reassurance that as a mere human he cannot ever mess up divine plans. He's just not that awesome. And while you and I are made in the image of the Almighty, His power forever extends beyond our own. God's plans are not subject to our abilities to carry them out.

In fact, God implies that He gifted us specifically to be able to experience His plans for our lives as we pursue relationship with Him. That includes *our lack* of certain gifting as well. Look at what God tells Moses next in Exodus 4:11–12:

> Then the LORD said to him, "Who has made man's mouth? Who makes him mute, or deaf, or seeing, or blind? Is it not I, the LORD? Now therefore go, and I will be with your mouth and teach you what you shall speak."

I love how God reminds Moses of His Name again!

Jesus also speaks about this gifting of God over our lives in the

Beatitudes in Matthew 5. He reminded us that no one lights a lamp and puts it "under a basket." What does Jesus mean? Jesus puts His light within us. Jesus made the way for the Holy Spirit to enter our lives and gift us for divine purposes. Jesus will not waste this light He has brought into our lives. He will use the gifting He gave us to impact others' lives. Will we believe He has a plan to help us overcome our fear of inadequacy and authenticate the calling He has issued us? Will we stop striving to prove our worth and attempt on our own to secure outcomes? Will we surrender to His divine plans for us?

God made your mind, your mouth, your heart, your hands all with great purpose. He does not look down from heaven and shake His head and think, "Well, shoot, I wish I would have made her a little smarter. I didn't realize she would be facing this circumstance at this point in her life. I'm just not sure she's got what it takes for the task I had in mind!" God does not suddenly regret how He made us because a circumstance takes Him by surprise.

Moses demands assurance that God can control the outcome He promises. Even if Moses messes up. Even if Moses does not have what it takes. No matter what circumstances unfold. God insists He can and that He will.

Fear reigns when we persist in limiting God's power. Moses respected God, he recognized God as greater than himself, but he still did not realize God's limitless power. In this exchange Moses doubts whether God can truly *make good* on His promises. He already doubted if God would *be good* on his behalf. This fear erupts in the right set of circumstances. And if there is something that often feels beyond our ability to control, our circumstances often rise to the top of the list.

When life becomes fairly routine and predictable we might forget our fear of inadequacy. But when something new occurs, our circumstances shift, and we require new courses of action, our fear resurfaces.

I taught elementary school for twelve years. I taught Sunday school for three years before that. I loved working with children. I never once walked into my classroom wondering if I had the skills to handle the day. I woke up excited to go to work. But when the nurse handed me Eliana in the hospital as I sat in the wheelchair ready to be taken from the safety of the hospital to my new life, I felt a surge of panic in my gut. *I don't know how to take care of a newborn! What if I can't get her to stop crying? What if I can't soothe her to sleep?* A thousand "what ifs" raced through my mind.

When we need to do something new or in a new way, we plague our minds with questions of self-doubt. After Nathan's birth the questions sounded only slightly different. "Sure, I can take care of one newborn, but can I swing a newborn and a toddler?" I remember taking him to the pediatrician for the first time and telling the doctor, "I know Eliana isn't even two years old yet, but please treat me like a first-time mom who doesn't know anything, because that's exactly how I feel!" And with each of my children being different in their personalities, preferences, and needs, I indeed was a first-time mom to Nathan. New seasons, new self-doubts.

> THERE ARE MOMENTS IN LIFE WHEN OUR FEAR OF INADEQUACY COMES TO FRUITION—WE JUST DON'T HAVE WHAT IT TAKES TO GET THROUGH.

We've heard the old adage that the only constant is change. These constant shifts in our circumstances leave us wondering if we can successfully adapt. Many studies have shown that a high percent of people will struggle with a fear of inadequacy at some point in their lives. It can be from having a second child, a suddenly sick child, a child with ongoing nontraditional needs. A new job. A move across country. A change in finances. Our child's move up to middle school. Having a parent or grandparent needing new levels of care. These circumstances challenge our fortitude and our faith. Will God be enough to get us through this new season? Can we learn to let Him be God in our lives?

When Cami's beautiful daughter Bella was diagnosed with cancer, Cami crumbled. She initially vowed to fight for her daughter's health with every last ounce of energy. Their friends, family, and church rallied around them with meals, transportation assistance with their older sons, and notes of encouragement. The months raged on and little four-year-old Bella with her once thick, curly black hair and sparkling eyes to match, bravely faced chemotherapy. But the weariness set in and the day came when Cami finally broke. She opened a care package someone sent to Bella. She pulled out a pink princess hairbrush and wept.

She suddenly felt entirely alone and ill-equipped to be brave for her little girl. A hairbrush? Had this person not seen the devastating Facebook post of a pink headband around Bella's bald head with the little girl forcing a weak smile for the camera? In that moment, Cami felt entirely alone in her fight. Cami knew she wanted to fight against Bella's cancer, but watching her little girl suffer she could not do. It crushed her. In this aspect of the battle, Cami was beaten. How do you prepare yourself to be the mother of a cancer patient? There are moments in life when our fear of inadequacy comes to fruition—we just don't have what it takes to get through. And even though God may have prepared us for our difficulties, when they come to pass it is He alone who carries us through.

God did carry Cami through. And beautiful Bella. Her curly black hair grew back and the sparkle in her eyes returned. But when you ask Cami, "How did you do it?" she tells you this: "I didn't. God did. There was no way I could have done this on my own. We had lots of people who helped us, but in the end, God's grace got us to the other side of this."

God in His great mercy prepares Moses for these difficult circumstances. Yet, Moses still insists he is unable to take this assignment from God. He tried to convince God he did not have the skill set, but God reminded him that every single one of Moses' skills or lack thereof had come from God Himself. Moses continues to defer and pleads with the Lord to send someone else to do it. Sometimes our fear of inadequacy drives us to rebellion.

Moses prefers to defer. And God allows it. "Then the anger of the LORD was kindled against Moses and he said, 'Is there not Aaron, your brother, the Levite? I know that he can speak well. . . . He shall speak for you to the people" (Ex. 4:14, 16). But Moses will discover just how deadly deferral can be. When God hands us an assignment that feels like a 97–page pdf and we want to walk away or hand it off to someone else, we need to remember God's limitless power over our lack. He will make good on His promises and be good on our behalf. He will be enough. And no matter how inadequate we may feel, or even how ill-equipped we may actually be, God's power and plan will prevail.

# *Intentional Trekking*

## Bible Reading Plan:
Exodus 4:1–17

## Truths for the Journey

- Our God is in the business of doing new things, which often means He does them in new ways.

- God created you to find life's fullest meaning in relationship with Him.

- No human will ever be powerful enough to thwart divine plans.

- God gave you your gifting for great purpose.

- We need to remember God's limitless power over our lack.

- God will make good on His promises and be good on our behalf.

## Processing the Journey

1. What is something you're not very good at and you've made peace with that fact?

2. How does realizing God purposefully gave us gifts, and left us areas of lack, change our perspective over our inabilities?

3. How does a proper perspective of God diminish our fear of inadequacy?

4. Do you struggle more to believe that God holds the power to make good on His promises or the character to be good on your behalf?

5. Have you ever been afraid you might mess up God's plans? How does knowing you are not powerful enough to thwart Him bring you comfort?

## Passionate Prayer

*Dear Jesus, help me trust You to make good on Your promises and to be good on my behalf. Help me to remember that You have never deferred Your sovereignty over to me. Your good and perfect plans are not subject to my ability to carry them out. Help me rest in Your authority and remember that You know both my strengths and my weaknesses. Help me remember You are the Lord, and there is nothing outside of Your wisdom or control.*

## CHAPTER FIVE

# Squashing Fears

*So he threw it on the ground, and it became a serpent,*

*and Moses ran from it.*

*Exodus 4:3*

When our kids were little, they used to love to catch lizards. Living in Arizona, we'd come across a slithering Lizzy nearly every time we went outside. One morning, my daughter rescued a two-inch-long baby lizard from the swimming pool. She tenderly placed it into a 9-by-13-inch Tupperware container and set it on the edge of the patio table in the sunlight. My three-year-old son, who moved only at the speed of light yet without the same level of precision, accidentally knocked the container over, and in a rapid attempt to grab the baby lizard, stepped on her, crushing her instantly. This wasn't the first time his boundless force broke something or brought destruction. In utter horror over his mistake, he ran away and hid under his bed sobbing, fearing the wrath of his sister.

About a week later I went into Nathan's room to put his laundry away. When I opened his sock drawer, I immediately reeled from a horrific odor. What in the world was buried underneath those

Superman socks? I spread them around and discovered a neatly folded paper towel with something inside. Squashed Lizzy.

"I thought maybe if we could bury Lizzy, then Sissy might not be so mad about it," he suggested. "I wanted her to know I was really sorry." But when you're three years old, sometimes you forget your well-intentioned plans. And Lizzy rots in your sock drawer.

Nathan initially responded to fear over his failure by running away. Then he hid that fear in a drawer, meaning to deal with it later, but forgetting to do so. Moses did the same thing. He enacted his personal Operation Deliverance by killing an Egyptian overseer. It didn't work out as planned, so he fled to Midian. He ran away. Since he hadn't moved on from Midian in forty years, I'm going to assume that Moses buried his failure in his sock drawer or his tent trunk, or whatever, also. But as the smell from Nathan's sock drawer proved, running away never makes it go away.

> TO CONQUER OUR FEAR AND SEE GOD'S POWER OVER IT, WE HAVE TO FACE IT. RUNNING AWAY ONLY MAKES US MORE FEARFUL.

Moses recounts to God what happened the last time he tried to convince the people of Israel that he was supposed to deliver them. "Then Moses answered, 'But behold, they will not believe me or listen to my voice, for they will say, 'The LORD did not appear to you.'" (Ex. 4:1).

Moses fears the people will not accept him as the chosen deliverer sent by God. He is certain they will question his calling and his capabilities. God forces Moses to face his fear head-on as He performs the miracle of turning the staff into a snake. But look at Moses' reaction and see what God tells him to do.

> The LORD said to him, "What is that in your hand?" He said, "A staff." And he said, "'Throw it on the ground." So he threw it on the ground, and it became a serpent, and Moses ran from it. But the LORD said to Moses, "Put out your hand and catch it by the tail"—so he put out his hand and caught it, and it became a

staff in his hand—"that they may believe that the LORD . . . has appeared to you."—Exodus 4:2–5

Through this sign, God taught Moses that not only could God empower him to face his fear, He could also equip Moses to conquer and subdue it. God did not turn the serpent back into a staff while Moses stood at a distance and watched. Once Moses fled from the snake, he had to turn around and return to the place of fear, snatch the serpent with his hand, and subdue it. To conquer our fear and see God's power over it, we have to face it. Running away only makes us more fearful.

The principal at Kelly's children's school desperately needed to mobilize their parent volunteers. With lots of parents concerned over the bullying incidents that had recently occurred on the playground, the teachers needed additional eyes and ears in the lunchroom and outside during recess. Kelly's children had collectively attended the school for almost ten years and lots of families knew her in the community.

"Would you please consider mobilizing the parents to take lunch hour shifts for the next three months? We need to reestablish faith in our school to protect our children," the principal pleaded. Kelly waffled. Who was she to be able to convince angry parents to become part of the solution rather than gossiping about the problem?

Kelly feared parents' backlash if she stood by the principal's side on this. What parent wanted to be told her child was causing problems? The principal persisted. "You have a background in human resources. You understand how to build teams and cast vision. And the parents like you. The school needs you."

Kelly dismissed the principal's perception of her capabilities immediately, saying, "I just processed applications and trained people from a manual. I'm not a leader. I'm not the person you need."

Kelly discounted her previous accomplishments, chalking them up to external factors that had nothing to do with her capabilities. "Cast vision"? No. She couldn't mobilize parents and rally them around a new cause: a better school for their community. Kelly began to avoid being on campus as much as possible. She wanted to run away so she wouldn't have to face her principal or her children's teachers. Nor did she want to listen to the parents complain or gossip about kids continuing to be bullied.

Kelly wrestled with her feeling of inadequacy to implement the principal's plan on behalf of the school. She could not see how her previous work history provided the skill set needed to solve this problem. Someone else should be asked, someone who would do it better. Eventually Kelly began to feel physically ill every time she came by the school and even toyed with fleeting thoughts of having her children transfer to a different school so she could be out of the picture.

Moses' default in fear is to flee. He prefers to defer rather than step into his assignment. To move past our fear of inadequacy, we have to turn around and face our fear. Sometimes we'll start striving in another direction in hopes to move further away from the problem. But God wants us to surrender the fear over to Him and allow Him to deal with it. God shows Moses that He is intent on helping him overcome with courage instead of flee in fright. Fearing others' responses to our failure causes us to run and hide. Moses preferred obscurity and tried to defer his position of leadership to his brother Aaron.

After Moses continually argued with God about his ability to take on this assignment, pleading with God to give it to someone else, God suggested Aaron become Moses' spokesman. But note carefully what God also said. "He shall speak for you to the people, and he shall be your mouth, and you shall be as God to him. *And take in your hand this staff, with which you shall do the signs*" (Ex. 4:16–17).

It was that same staff God made him face in fear, and made him subdue and squash. Aaron speaks, Moses performs the signs. Got it. Except that's not what happened. And God made extra sure Moses understood His directions, because He repeats them a second time:

"And the LORD said to Moses, 'When *you* go back to Egypt, see that *you* do before Pharaoh all the miracles that I have put in *your* power'" (Ex 4:21a). Those "yous" and that "your" are not plural. God did not mean Moses and Aaron. He meant Moses.

But look what happens when Moses gets back to Egypt:

> And Moses told Aaron all the words of the LORD with which He had sent him to speak, and all the signs that he had commanded him to do. Then Moses and Aaron went and gathered together all the elders of the people of Israel. *Aaron spoke all the words that the LORD had spoken to Moses and did the signs in the sight of the people.*—Exodus 4:28–31

Wait, what? I thought Aaron was supposed to speak and Moses was supposed to perform the miracles.

Up to this point, it appears that Aaron is doing everything and Moses is basically standing there along for the ride. He takes a backseat to his older brother. But this isn't the arrangement God intended. Our fear propels us into passivity, but God invites us to intentionally pursue victory.

Kelly became increasingly passive regarding the bullying problems at school. But eventually God brought them home to her when her own daughter was cornered in the bathroom. Kelly despised the idea of being the school's front face of an anti-bullying campaign and desperately sought someone else to head up the program though she said she'd help out. If the program failed, as she suspected it would, she didn't want to be the one responsible.

Our fear of inadequacy will cause us to hide behind others, deflecting the outcome onto them, so we won't be responsible for any future failures. But God doesn't want us to sit back and miss out on what He has planned for us, so He addresses Moses' unwillingness to follow His commands.

Not only does God deal with Moses' default to flee, He also brings him face to face with his fear of rejection. God's heart includes freeing us from our fears, so He orchestrates circumstances forcing us to face those fears. People were not cooperative and did not support his efforts, precisely what he feared would happen. When placed in the right set of circumstances, that old serpent slithers close and hisses in our ear, "See, I knew you'd fail. Why do you even try?"

Moses and Aaron go and confront Pharaoh. They ask the king of Egypt to kindly grant a few days' vacation from brickmaking for the Israelite slaves that they may go worship God in the wilderness. Pharaoh scoffs over such a suggestion. "I don't know your God— why would I let your people go? Get back to work."

Then Pharaoh takes the matter further. He punishes the Israelites. "The same day Pharaoh commanded the taskmasters of the people and their foremen, 'You shall no longer give the people straw to make bricks, as in the past; let them go and gather straw for themselves. But the number of bricks that they made in the past you shall impose on them'" (Ex. 5:6–8).

The Israelites proved unable to collect straw and still produce the same number of bricks.

> And the foremen of the people of Israel, whom Pharaoh's taskmasters had set over them, were beaten and were asked, "Why have you not done all your task of making bricks today and yesterday, as in the past?"—Exodus 5:14

Let's think about this. During Moses' first attempt at Operation Deliverance he witnessed an Egyptian beating a Hebrew *in front of* him. And in anger, Moses killed the Egyptian and hid him in the sand. Now Moses witnesses many Hebrews being beaten *because of him.* His confrontation with Pharaoh resulted in more than a redo of his initial attempt. It made the situation worse. Talk about the perfect circumstance for his fear of inadequacy to erupt!

The foremen met with Moses and Aaron and they were not happy. "The LORD look on you and judge," they said, "because you have made us stink in the sight of Pharaoh and his servants, and have put a sword in their hand to kill us" (Ex. 5:21). The people reject Moses and express their anger and blame toward him. Moses in turn responds to God: "Why did you ever send me? For since I came to Pharaoh to speak in your name, he has done evil to this people, and you have not delivered your people at all" (vv. 22–23).

Did this come as a surprise to God? Why did He let events unfold in this manner? Why did God cause the very thing Moses feared most to be what actually happened?

Could it be that just as He showed Moses he did not have to run in fear from the serpent, neither did he need to run in fear from the serpent's lies? Moses faced rejection. He heard those words spoken by the Israelites, which no doubt pierced him deeply. He complains to the Lord over it. But he pressed on. He faced the fear and continued to obey. We may not have to tangibly tackle a serpent, but we will battle his insidious suggestions that our only future is failure. God may allow us to experience rejection so we learn that once we've walked through it and pressed on in His power, those lies of the enemy no longer sound so ominous.

> GOD MAY ALLOW US TO EXPERIENCE REJECTION SO WE LEARN THAT ONCE WE'VE WALKED THROUGH IT AND PRESSED ON IN HIS POWER, THOSE LIES OF THE ENEMY NO LONGER SOUND SO OMINOUS.

Kelly eventually found a core group of parents to catch the vision. The lunchroom added needed staff and the children doing the bullying stopped. The result didn't come without a lot of frustration on Kelly's part, but the problem eventually was resolved and the parents regained faith in the school's ability to protect the children. Kelly felt God's presence with her each time she stepped on school grounds.

What opportunities, circumstances or situations do you avoid out of fear of inadequacy or rejection? It's time to grab it by the tail and squash it in your fist. Running away will never make it go away. If God has placed this person or position in your path, maybe it's time to stop running, turn around, and face your fear. When the enemy slithers close, silence those hisses with the truth that your God knows the playbook. Even moments of rejection hold purpose.

And that failure you've tucked away in your sock drawer that you meant to deal with and then forgot? It's time to give Squashed Lizzy a proper burial.

# *Intentional Trekking*

## Bible Reading Plan:
Exodus 4:18–23, 27–31; 5:1–23

## Truths for the Journey

- Running away doesn't make our fear of inadequacy go away.
- Sometimes to move past our fear of inadequacy we have to turn around and face our fear.
- God can empower us to face our fear and equip us to conquer and subdue it.
- God intends to help us overcome in courage rather than flee in fright.
- Our fear propels us into passivity, but God invites us to intentionally pursue victory.
- Even moments of rejection hold purpose.

## Processing the Journey

1. What types of circumstances cause you to flee because you prefer not to deal with them?

2. What is a mistake you have made that you prefer to keep buried?

3. Why do you think God forced Moses to grab the serpent by the tail in order for it to change back into a staff rather than just snap his finger or issue a verbal command?

4. Have you ever deferred responsibility over to someone else because it felt safer or easier? How does shirking responsibility signify a fear of inadequacy and potential failure?

5. What is a circumstance or a relationship in which the enemy hisses that your only future is failure? How do the life lessons God teaches Moses in this passage of Scripture encourage you?

## Passionate Prayer

*Dear Jesus, help me stop deferring and hiding behind others. Give me courage to step forward in faith and follow You in obedience. Help me believe that when I am obeying You, I will never fail, for my obedience is what You desire of me most. Help me to face my fears and stop running away from people and situations that You are calling me to hand over to You in faith. Give me wisdom to know what I need to let go of and what I need to conquer by Your power.*

## CHAPTER SIX

# Outward Signs of Inward Belief

*And Moses took the staff of God in his hand.*

*Exodus 4:20*

I have a copy of a book my dad wrote on my desk. It sits right in front of me every time I sit down to write anything—an article, an email, or a book. I probably won't ever even open it (sorry, Dad!) because the idea of three hundred-plus pages of *The Complete Handbook of Maintenance Management* sounds more like a cure for insomnia than a casual read. But nonetheless it sits before me at all times. Why? Because whenever my fear of inadequacy erupts within, taunting me with things like, "*Why do you even waste your time writing this? No one cares what you have to say! And you aren't even a good writer! Give it up already!*" I look at my dad's book.

I mean, glance at *The Complete Handbook of Maintenance Management* and who would not think those same thoughts? Who in their right mind would ever want to read *that*? And I vividly envision my dad getting his manuscript back in the mail, with more red ink on the page than black, despondently shaking his head while sitting down to rework it. *Again*. But he finished. And over 300,000 people have read it. Professors from all over the world taught from it. So I'm guessing the writing ended up being pretty darn good. *Because he refused to listen to the lies of inadequacy and persisted.*

My dad's book serves as a tangible reminder to persevere. I can remember my dad editing my high school papers the same way. He covered the thing with scrawl, teaching me to write more tightly. I can still hear him commanding, "Focus on the verbs! Those are the most powerful words in your sentence." When the enemy slithers close and snarls, *"Who cares? No one cares! No one will want to read that!"* I glance at dad's big blue book with fancy gold letters and think, "Millions of people probably won't, but maybe thirty will, and maybe God will comfort them through my words." And I persist.

Sometimes in our journey with God we need tangible reminders that God is with us. For Moses, gripping the staff in his hand reinforced God's presence with Him. God planned it that way.

"And take in your hand this staff, with which you shall do the signs" (Ex. 4:17). When Moses set out from Midian to return to Egypt that staff became his mainstay. "So Moses took his wife and his sons and had them ride on a donkey, and went back to the land of Egypt. *And Moses took the staff of God in his hand*" (Ex. 4:20).

The staff previously served as Moses' identity as a shepherd. How beautiful that God used this same instrument to help Moses reframe God's plan for him: to become the shepherd of His people, Israel!

God would work through Moses' staff to inflict plagues on their captor, part the Red Sea for their escape, communicate battle plans against their enemies, provide water for their thirst, bring healing against diseases. This tangible object exemplified God's power and His presence. Gripping this staff within his hand no doubt proved comforting to Moses on many occasions as he recounted the miracles God worked through it. A tangible reminder of God's presence with him and His faithfulness toward him.

My friend Sammi keeps tangible reminders of God's presence and faithfulness up and down her arms. For years Sammi battled drug addiction, and the track marks of scars remain before her always. You might think she would prefer to keep them covered, because they certainly would not be considered beautiful to most people who view them. But she rarely wears long sleeves. Those track marks serve as tangible reminders of the power and faithfulness of God in her life.

Sometimes God's tangible reminders can be objects, but primarily God uses people. My dad's big blue book serves as a combination of both, especially since my dad is no longer here with us. But I can imagine in my head what he would say if I uttered aloud thoughts of quitting. (I'll spare you that, because my Marine Corps officer father needed a tea towel in his kitchen that said, "I really love Jesus but I still cuss a little!") While the staff symbolized Moses' role as a shepherd-in-Midian-turned-deliverer-and-shepherd of Israel, God will use people to frame Moses' identity as God's child.

Moses begins to identify with his Israelite heritage in this next discourse. Look carefully at how he describes the people of Israel to his father-in-law Jethro: "Please let me go back to *my brothers* in Egypt to see whether they are still alive" (Ex. 4:18). Moses begins using relational language to describe Israel. Let's compare this with how God describes Israel.

> Then you shall say to Pharaoh, "Thus says the LORD, *Israel is my firstborn son,* and I say to you, 'Let *my son* go that he may serve me.' If you refuse to let him go, behold, I will kill your firstborn son."—Exodus 4:22–23

God also uses relational language.

But while Moses refers to Israel as his brothers, he still wavers in identification with his people, because Moses had not performed the primary act of identification of an Israelite with his sons: circumcision. Keeping a blue book on your desk seems a whole lot simpler, but God instituted this plan several hundred years earlier through Abraham in Genesis 17 in order to demonstrate to Israel in a very tangible way that God's covenant with His people passed down from generation to generation beginning at conception.

In a strange twist of events, God almost kills "Alien" or Moses' son Gershom, because he was not circumcised, until Moses' wife does some quick thinking and performs the act in the middle of their journey. We see Moses exhibiting some outward signs that he believes God through his obedience to God's game plan, but we also see him holding back from full identification with God's people.

Only partially putting ourselves out there commonly occurs when we are still battling our fear of inadequacy. We find other purposeful pursuits to consume our time so we easily justify not obeying God.

Right after God refers to Israel as His firstborn son, read what happens next during Moses' trip back to Egypt: "At a lodging place on the way the LORD met him and sought to put him to death. Then Zipporah took a flint and cut off her son's foreskin [that is, circumcised him] and touched Moses' feet with it . . . So he [God] let him alone" (Ex. 4:24–26).

WHILE TANGIBLE ITEMS CAN PROVE COMFORTING TO US IN DIFFICULT MOMENTS OF INADEQUACY, GOD MOST OFTEN USES PEOPLE TO HELP US PROPERLY FRAME OUR IDENTITY AS HIS CHILDREN.

God commanded Israelite fathers to circumcise their sons, and if they failed to do so, God threatened their death. While it seems strange that Moses finally obeys God and heads back to Egypt only to have God threaten to kill him on the way, I think this striking series of events proved comforting to him.

While Moses may not have fully identified himself as a child of God, this stern visit from God solidified God's view of him. Gershom indeed was a sojourner in a strange land, or an "alien," because as Moses' firstborn son, he was an Israelite, not a son of Midian. God uses Moses' wife Zipporah to show him his true identity—a true Israelite, one of God's chosen people. While tangible items such as a staff or a big blue book can prove comforting to us in difficult moments of inadequacy, God most often uses people to help us properly frame our identity as His children. God instituted the church, the family of God, to serve as tangible reminders of God's promises. Fear tells us to guard and isolate ourselves from others because they might reject or harm us. Our fear of inadequacy slithers close and hisses, "Rejection is certain when others realize who you really are!" But God commands us to commit to our fellow kingdom citizens. Not just outwardly, but inwardly as well, to consider their lives as our own, to view them as "my brothers." As we look around at our lives, with whom do we identify? Are we intentionally building relationships within the family of God or are we identifying with groups speaking alternative identities into our lives?

Julie struggled to find friends at church. Juggling her family responsibilities along with work left her out of many of the women's activities. Many events took place during the day when she couldn't attend. She signed up for an exercise class at the gym, which met in the late afternoon three days a week, convenient for her to attend on the way home from her job. She began to connect with some other working women whom she saw regularly in her fitness classes. None of them had any sort of relationship with God, and their workout routines ruled their lives. Her new friends started attending an additional workout session on Sunday mornings and begged Julie to join them. At first, she felt guilty skipping church and only watching it online, but after slipping in and out of the service with no one even acknowledging her presence, Julie easily justified her absence.

After a few months, her workout tribe decided to start entering half-marathons and going on girls' trips. Julie felt she had earned the challenge after faithfully putting so many hours toward her exercise routine. While her husband, Tim, applauded her new physique, he began to notice a shift in her attitude. She began to obsess over her fitness. She became annoyed when the kids' activities interfered with her workout routines. She spent more and more time at the

LETTING GOD BE ENOUGH

gym, leaving the kids home alone after school for longer periods of
time. Her husband took the kids to church without her and started
to resent feeling like a single dad while she was off with others.

> GOD ALONE FRAMES OUR
> IDENTITY BECAUSE WE
> BELONG TO HIM. HE IS
> OUR FATHER. AND OUR
> BROTHERS AND SISTERS
> BECOME THE PEOPLE
> GOD USES TO REMIND US
> OF THAT FACT.

Eventually Tim called their pastor,
who pointed them to a Christian marriage
counselor and helped the couple set some
boundaries. Julie felt like she had finally
found friends, and these relationships
became extremely important to her. She
forgot her identity as a child of God. Julie and
Tim started going to a small group, and Julie
began to build friendships with some other
women at church. She immediately noticed
the joy in these women compared to the constant complaining she
experienced with her gym friends. While she continued to go to
exercise classes and occasionally participate in races, Julie regained
her true identity as a follower of Christ, bringing balance back into
her life when she was no longer so desperate for acceptance from
an unhealthy group of friends. God used the body of Christ to help
Julie understand her true identity.

Zipporah somehow instinctively knew Moses' true identity and
acted to confirm it. As believers in Jesus Christ, our primary identity
also becomes "Child of God" or "Kingdom Citizen"—different ways
of saying the same thing. God alone frames our identity because
we belong to Him. He is our Father. And our brothers and sisters
become the people God uses to remind us of that fact. They teach
us the Word. They pray for clarity. They call out lies we may have
unintentionally come to believe about God and about ourselves.

Our fear of inadequacy grows when other relationships become
preeminent in framing our identity. Our non-believing coworkers.
Our workout tribe. News anchors. Social media pundits. Self-
serving bosses. Dysfunctional family members. Even wounded Jesus
followers. Yes, even the family of God sometimes mars our identity.

But God's plan remains. As each member sees Him more clearly, we see ourselves more clearly, and become equipped to remind each other of our true identity.

Look at how the apostle Paul describes the family of God and God's plan for it to shape us:

> And he gave the apostles, the prophets, the evangelists, the shepherds and teachers, to equip the saints for the work of ministry, for building up the body of Christ, until we all attain to the unity of the faith and of the knowledge of the Son of God, to mature manhood, to the measure of the stature of the fullness of Christ, so that we may no longer be children, tossed to and fro by the waves and carried about by every wind of doctrine, by human cunning, by craftiness in deceitful schemes. Rather, speaking the truth in love, we are to grow up in every way into him who is the head, into Christ, from whom the whole body, joined and held together by every joint with which it is equipped, when each part is working properly, makes the body grow so that it builds itself up in love.—Ephesians 4:11–16

Look at the roles of God's family in helping us overcome our fear of inadequacy! Remember where this fear remains rooted: an imperception of God's power and lack of intimacy with His character. What does the family of God afford us in reframing our view of God and thus ourselves?

We become built up.

We grow in our knowledge of Christ and move toward unity.

We become mature.

We practice discernment when false identities are spoken over us or the enemy snarls in our ear.

We speak the truth to one another in love and point out when a fear of inadequacy diminishes our perception of God's power or deteriorates His character.

Each person shares in the work of pointing their fellow family members toward a greater understanding of Christ and our identity as His children.

While our fear of inadequacy forces us to isolate, God's plan to conquer this fear comes through community. The subtle whispers of our enemy shout most loudly when we are alone. God used a staff to bring Moses comfort, but He used people to help Moses understand his true identity. Look at Zipporah's response to Moses—"Surely you are a bridegroom of blood to me!" (Ex. 4:25). I don't exactly know how to translate that into relatable vernacular, but I don't think it was a compliment. She sounds pretty harsh. Sometimes God may be reframing our identity through difficult truth or even unkind words.

Our enemy wants to isolate us so we only hear his hisses of inadequacy. Once he isolates us, he generally leads us to a new relationship or set of relationships that pull us further away from our relationship with Christ. God longs to teach us our true identity through the community of His people. Even when their words might be harsh (maybe even a cuss word or two, Dad!). God in His great mercy provides objects of comfort to remind us of His presence with us and His faithfulness toward us. God uses our brothers and sisters to grow us up into discerning family members who build others up. And while the methods may prove messy (ahem, circumcision!), the means build perseverance. We refuse to listen to the lies of our enemy and, instead, persist just like my Jesus-loving, sometimes-cussing Dad.

# Intentional Trekking

## Bible Reading Plan:
Exodus 4:17–26

## Truths for the Journey

- Sometimes in our journey with God we need tangible reminders that God is with us.

- Sometimes God's tangible reminders can be objects, but God primarily uses people.

- God alone frames our identity. He is our Father.

- Our primary identity is child of God.

- God instituted the church, the family of God, to remind us of our identity.

- Our fear of inadequacy is rooted in an imperception of God's power and lack of intimacy with His character.

- The subtle whispers of our enemy shout most loudly when we are alone.

- Sometimes God may reframe our identity through difficult truth or even unkind words.

## Processing the Journey

1. Do you have a tangible object that brings you comfort? What is it and of what does it remind you?

2. Is there a person in your life who has influenced your identity negatively? How so?

3. Is there a believer in your life who has influenced your identity positively? What specifically did they do to help reframe your identity as a child of God?

4. Why do you think God created community to be the means which shapes our identity?

5. If we refuse to commit to community, who else suffers besides just ourselves according to Ephesians 4?

6. What is one practical step you can take to begin to commit to community with God's people, even though you may have previously experienced being wounded by one of them?

## Passionate Prayer

*Dear Jesus, please forgive me for pulling away from Your people.*
*Help me trust that You have decided to form my identity*
*through community. Even when their words may be harsh*
*or painful. Even then You can use their rejection for my*
*construction—to make me more like You. Forgive me when*
*I see the unfairness of others but fail to see where my own*
*actions have wounded others. Help me remember that when*
*I am serving Your family, Jesus, I am serving You.*
*And You are oh, so worthy.*

## CHAPTER SEVEN

# *Dealing with Disappointment*

*"For since I came to Pharaoh to speak in your name, he has done evil to this people, and you have not delivered your people at all."*

*Exodus 5:23*

My dad never sat still very well. So, in preparation for when he and my mom came to visit, Jonathan and I would stockpile a to-do list around the house and yard. My dad loved to be needed, and with his rigorous work week, my husband loved the help at home, so it served as a win-win for everyone. One summer we noticed my dad's fatigue immediately. Normally he would knock out three or four projects a day, stopping only for a sandwich. This summer he slept in. He took naps. He sat down a lot. Something was wrong. We implored him to go to the doctor for testing. About a month later we discovered the problem. My dad had multiple myeloma, sort of like cancer in your blood. The prognosis was not good. Jonathan and I immediately began to pray about moving closer to my parents.

A job offer came quickly. Our house sold in days. We sensed so many signs that God was leading us back out west. Over and over I felt, "If I can just get out there, everything will be okay!" Except it wasn't. Jonathan's job failed to pan out the way we had expected, and his stress level left him frazzled. My parents still felt far away even though we had shrunk a seven-hour flight to a three-hour drive. I sat at home with a two- and three-year old, desperately lonely, all of us missing our friends, and scared to lose my dad. We wondered if we had misunderstood God's directions.

Moses knew Pharaoh wasn't going to listen to him. He expected that. What he didn't expect was that things would get worse for the people of Israel before they got better. Moses thought that if he obeyed God, then everything would be good. God would deliver the people and protect them from Pharaoh until He made good on His promise. But the plan backfires. Remember the whole change in the brick-making quota thing? And the Israelite foremen get beaten by their Egyptian taskmasters? Moses is disappointed. And disillusioned. And he complains to God.

> Then Moses turned to the LORD and said, "O Lord, why have you done evil to this people? Why did you ever send me? For since I came to Pharaoh to speak in your name, he has done evil to this people, and you have not delivered your people at all."—Exodus 5:22–23

Nothing escalates our fear of inadequacy like unexpected circumstances. When we finally muster up enough courage to take a step forward and the ground falls out beneath us, we reel backward, vowing never to be so foolish again. Moses finally obeyed God and returned to Egypt. He announced—well, Aaron announced—his arrival to the people of Israel. He appeared before Pharaoh in a heated confrontation. But it all backfires. The people reject him. Pharaoh worsens their condition, and Moses wonders why he was dumb enough to attempt Operation Deliverance a second time.

What Moses didn't see was how this seeming setback actually worked to help mobilize the people and facilitate their communication. Think about it. Previously, each Israelite is located in one place, either making their bricks or assembling the building with an Egyptian overseer watching and listening at all times. But now the Israelites are scattered. And they are supposed to be! Think of how greatly this would aid their communication with one another. Those straw-gatherers could serve as messengers to disseminate Moses' directions to them. And warn them of what plagues would come and when.

The straw gathering debacle also undoubtedly became a catalyst for them to heed Moses' directions with greater urgency, wishing to escape their current oppressors. Their difficult labor escalated to oppressive and impossible, possibly increasing their excitement over God's promised deliverance from their circumstances. But Moses did not see any of this. Instead he saw evil flourishing and freedom fading away for the Israelites.

One thing Moses got right in his disappointment, however, was his choice to turn to God. Look at how God answers Moses in the opening of Exodus 6 concerning His plans for the Israelites in the middle of this mess:

> "Now you shall see what I will do to Pharaoh; for with a strong hand he will send them out, and with a strong hand he will drive them out of his land."—Exodus 6:1

God reminded Moses of the covenant He had made with his ancestors, promising them a new land of their own. He also reminded Moses that "I have heard the groaning of the people of Israel whom the Egyptians hold as slaves."

God sums up with unambiguous statements:

"I am the LORD."

"I will bring you out from under the burdens of the Egyptians."

"I will deliver you from slavery to them."

The Egyptians among whom the Hebrews were living worshiped a whole array of gods as did the Canaanites, Babylonians, and other polytheistic cultures. A god's name explained his or her purpose or function. They had gods in charge of the weather, the crops, the sun, war, diseases, and even Geb, the god of dust! The gods in these cultures were motivated to aid humans so that humans in turn would help them. It was not for a relationship between Creator and created.

OUR FEAR OF INADEQUACY ERUPTS WHEN CIRCUMSTANCES SPIN OUT OF CONTROL. WE CAN, LIKE MOSES, THINK THAT IF A SITUATION IS HARD, THAT MEANS GOD IS NOT REALLY IN IT.

God explains to Moses in this exchange that as LORD, He is the Creator God, or the God who enters relationship. This function of Yahweh remained unique to Him. No other god existed for the sole purpose of having relationship with humans. God would function as Israel's deliverer for the purpose of building relationship with them.

Second, God explains to Moses a bit more clearly how Operation Deliverance will go down. Initially God told Moses back in Exodus 3:20 that He would deliver Israel through "all the wonders that I will do." This Hebrew word for wonders is *pala*. It means wondrous things, miracles, to separate, to consecrate, to make extraordinary, to act miraculously, to act marvelously, to sanctify.[9] Now I don't know what you imagine when you read those descriptors, but I certainly would not have envisioned the straw-gathering debacle and the beating of the Israelite slaves. I have a feeling that Moses thought he would return to Egypt and God would put on a spectacular show, releasing them from Pharaoh's grip. I don't think Moses thought it was going to be hard, especially on the Israelites who already were suffering.

After all, wasn't that the whole reason Moses was being sent in the first place? To deliver God's people out of difficult circumstances?

Our fear of inadequacy erupts when circumstances spin out of control. We can, like Moses, think that if a situation is hard, that means God is not really in it. When those around us feel the same way, our feelings of inadequacy escalate. Look at how the people responded to this message from God: "Moses spoke thus to the people of Israel, but they did not listen to Moses, because of their broken spirit and harsh slavery" (Ex. 6:9).

Instead of spurring the people to jump onboard the Operation Deliverance train, they too became defeated. They were overwhelmed by their circumstances just like Moses. But God explains to Moses what he had misunderstood regarding God's plans. Instead of God describing His acts as "wonders" as He did in Exodus 3, this time God said, "great acts of judgment" (Ex. 6:6).

This Hebrew word is *shaphat* and means to condemn, to contend with the notion of punishing, to punish the guilty, to give justice or equality.[10] *Yes, Moses, I am going to perform miracles, but they will be miracles of judgment against Pharaoh for his wicked treatment of my people. This isn't going to be a cakewalk, Moses. This is going to be tough. Don't expect all this to make sense to you. Keep running to Me with your questions!*

Handing over our fears to God means learning to accept what we cannot comprehend. It means we stop striving to make sense out of it and surrender in trust that God knows what He's doing. In Moses' fear of inadequacy, he falsely concluded that he was failing at his mission, yet again. Sometimes God's ways don't make sense to us, but as we grow in relationship with Him we begin to understand that what is mysterious often opens the door to the majestic. Just because we cannot see where God is headed doesn't mean He has stopped leading. And when God appears to be taking us backward, this doesn't mean we aren't ready to go forward.

Again, Moses' fear appears to be rooted in the circumstances, but a careful examination of his words to God reveal the real source of his insecurity. "The people of Israel have not listened to me. How then shall Pharaoh listen to me, for I am of uncircumcised lips?" (Ex. 6:12). Here we go again with the circumcision thing! Circumcision marked your identification as a true Israelite—a true chosen child of God. Moses' fear of inadequacy remains rooted in his lack of identity. Moses makes this argument *twice* before God. *I'm not really an Israelite. I'm not really one of Your chosen children.*

Usually our fear of inadequacy does not derive from difficulty. The stress of circumstances merely causes fear to surface. Our motivation behind endless striving roots itself in the hope that if we control our world, keeping it smooth and stable, our fear will cool. But in actuality fear remains and kindles hotter due to our frenetic activity. Eventually, given the right circumstances, that fear erupts, and because it usually took a tremendous amount of heat and stress to come to that point, we falsely assume the disappointment or the disaster caused the fear.

Moses' fear remains rooted in his imperception of God's power and lack of intimacy with His character. God is LORD—the God of relationship. Moses is His chosen child, and disappointing circumstances do not signify His displeasure, but rather depict the brokenness of life on this shattered planet. Sometimes God's plans unfold in ways we cannot comprehend, sending us reeling backward in confusion over His ways.

I mistakenly held the misconception that once we arrived in Arizona, everything with my dad would be okay. I placed my hope in a shift in circumstances rather than the security of an unchangeable God. My father did not improve. He worsened and only lived a few months after we arrived. My husband soon after discovered his need to seek new employment. There were many lonely days and lots of unanswered questions. I questioned why we had come.

Neither of us had any idea of all that God had in store for us. My dad's illness moved us to Arizona, but we arrived for much broader needs than we realized in the moment. We needed to be close to my mom to help her after Dad passed away. We needed our church family to grow deep spiritual roots for the future. Being in a state with so many transplants, we quickly forged friendships with people who became like family as we raised our children. God opened the door for Jonathan to fulfill his dream of owning his own practice. God brought us to Arizona, but not for the reasons we thought.

What seems like moving backward is actually a shortcut to the path we were meant to travel all along. Moses learned one of life's most valuable lessons regarding a relationship with God: being honest with God about his feelings. Notice how brutally honest Moses' words are to God! He does not circumvent his confusion or his frustration toward God over his circumstances. He tells God plainly how he feels.

> **WHAT SEEMS LIKE MOVING BACKWARD IS ACTUALLY A SHORTCUT TO THE PATH WE WERE MEANT TO TRAVEL ALL ALONG.**

This intimacy with our Father allows us to unload our doubts, questions, frustrations, and insecurities and provides the pathway to peace with our circumstances. Moses was able to come to a place of acceptance that God's plans were sometimes beyond his comprehension. He then began to develop a lifelong habit of turning to God in his disappointment.

Again, God promises to right this current wrong the people of Israel are experiencing.

> "I will take you to be my people, and I will be your God, and you shall know that I am the LORD your God, who has brought you out from under the burdens of the Egyptians. I will bring you into the land that I swore to give to Abraham, to Isaac, and to Jacob. I will give it to you for a possession. I am the LORD."—Exodus 6:7–8

God repeats the purpose, His win of the game: that His people are delivered, brought out of Egypt, and into the promised land where they experience, for the first time, true relationship with Him. Their identity will be rooted in Him—they are His chosen children. He will be their God and dwell in their midst, guiding, directing, and protecting them. Moses does not need to fix these disappointing circumstances. Moses needs to remember his God is the LORD and Moses is His child. I AM is unfolding His plans. But Moses does not grasp this yet. And if we're honest, when most of us experience confusing or disappointing circumstances, we do not see what I AM is doing either.

And here is the reason. Moses does not fully embrace his identity, calling himself "uncircumcised." Each one of us must come to our own place of decision. Will we believe what God says about Himself—that He is the Lord and desires intimacy with us?

Until we fully embrace these two truths—that we are created by and deeply loved by our Father and that we are designed to be in an eternal loving relationship with Him—we will continue to falter. Influenced by our circumstances and reeling in the winds of change, we will:

- default into self-doubt,
- debase our giftedness and value,
- declare our inability to carry out assignments God places upon us,
- distrust God's plan to demonstrate His kindness and goodness in our lives,
- disassociate from our primary identity as a chosen child of God,
- decide disappointing circumstances reflect God's displeasure over us, and
- define ourselves with roles, responsibilities, and relationships apart from God.

Nothing displayed my fear of inadequacy like those first few months after our arrival in Arizona. Between my husband's job, my dad's failing health, my mom's grief over my dad, and two toddlers, circumstances swirled around me like a fierce storm, threatening to knock me down. We could not see at all what God was doing. We thought we had followed His leading to Arizona, but the idea of going back to North Carolina felt so much simpler and safer. But Arizona rooted us in the exact church family we needed to get through this storm. We forged relationships with those who reminded us of our identity: chosen, children of God—kept in His care always—even when circumstances shouted otherwise. We wondered in the mess if we made a mistake, but God knew exactly what He was doing.

Will you turn to the Lord with your disappointments today, friend? Your Father longs for you to rest in His power and revel in His goodness. He knows what He's doing in your life.

# *Intentional Trekking*

## Bible Reading Plan:
Exodus 5–6

## Truths for the Journey

- We think that if we obey God, our circumstances will always be good.

- Nothing escalates our fear of inadequacy like unexpected circumstances.

- Handing over our fear to God means learning to accept what we cannot comprehend.

- As we grow in our relationship with God, we discover that what remains mysterious opens the door to the majestic.

- Just because we cannot see where God is headed does not mean He has stopped leading.

- Ultimately our fear of inadequacy remains rooted in our identity: we do not see ourselves as a chosen child of God.

- Disappointing circumstances do not signify God's displeasure.

## Processing the Journey

1. Have circumstances or outcomes unfolded in disappointment leaving you wondering if you had misunderstood God? Describe the situation and the emotions tied to it.

2. Why do you think we have a hard time when our obedience leads to disappointing or difficult circumstances?

3. What is a circumstance or relationship that you cannot understand but you have trusted God with it?

4. Do you tend to equate difficult circumstances as signs of God's displeasure?

5. Describe what you believe it means to have your identity as a chosen child of God. On a practical level, what does that look like in our daily lives?

6. Which of the points above can you relate to most and why?

## Passionate Prayer

*Dear Jesus, sometimes I struggle to know and understand
Your will. Sometimes You feel far away and mysterious.
Help me remember that Your ways are not like mine.
Your wisdom exceeds my understanding. I will never be able to
fully comprehend where and how You work Your wonderful
ways. Help me trust You nonetheless. Help me remember that
I am Your chosen child and am always in Your care.*

## CHAPTER **EIGHT**

# Dealing with Distractions

*And he went out from Pharaoh in hot anger.*

*Exodus 11:8*

My husband keeps his cool under fire. If the sky is going to fall or the earth crash under your feet, Jonathan is the guy you want next to you. He holds an uncanny ability to remain emotionally detached and objectively survey his circumstances, determining the wisest course of action. (In contrast, I'm a sanguine, emotional roller coaster, so he constitutes a perfect match.) It's a great quality to have as a surgeon and I'm sure he's had plenty of opportunities to use this gift in the operating room. But I vividly remember a time when my roll-with-the-punches guy threatened to throw around some punches instead.

Jonathan, my mom, and I spent the afternoon on a golf course. I am not a golfer, I merely came along to appease my husband and was definitely the weakest link on the chain. Designed for busy executives, you could walk this course since it was smaller than most, so Jonathan thought maybe my consistent hundred-yard drives could swing it. (If you're also not a golfer, that is a ridiculously short length for the ball to travel when teeing off!) Like I said, I am not a golfer and what should have taken two or three swings to sink the ball consistently took me four or five and the foursome behind us grew impatient. They started to pressure us.

Then came the final straw. While I futilely attempted to sink my final putt, the golf ball from one of the men in the group behind us whizzed inches from my face. And my husband lost it. Completely. He threw his putter across the green and defiantly marched toward the four men demanding their immediate departure from the course! My mom and I looked at each other, stunned. We had never seen him act like that before.

"Which one of you hit that ball?" he growled. "You could have killed my wife! What golf game is so important you are willing to put someone's life at risk? You have no business being on this course if you are going to behave so recklessly!" The foursome stood there frozen. "Get in your cart and get off this course right now or my fist is going to be in your face!" Jonathan threatened.

My mom, ever the Mama Bear herself, was right behind him echoing her own threats. The four men climbed into their cart in robotic fashion and drove back to the clubhouse.

In Exodus 11 we see Moses' anger get the best of him. First it was back in Egypt when he rashly murdered the Egyptian overseer. Now after a long contest with Pharaoh (many scholars suggest it was a span of months), we see Moses' anger erupt again.

Often, our anger and frustration actually stem from our fear of inadequacy and failure. When we experience a lack of control, a distrust of others, or angst over an outcome, anger and frustration emerge. Moses has gone head-to-head with Pharaoh at least fifteen times now and Pharaoh has stubbornly refused his requests, reneged on his promises, manipulated Moses to appease him, and wreaked complete havoc for the Egyptians. You might already be familiar with the story, and you'll be directed to it in this chapter's Bible reading plan. Briefly, God through Moses warned Pharaoh of plagues that would come upon the land if he refused to let the Israelites go, and Egypt experienced plagues of water being turned to blood, flies, darkness . . . you get the idea. After several requests to let the Israelites go and Pharaoh's emphatic refusals, God began to inflict plagues upon the Egyptians until Pharaoh finally relented after the tenth and final plague. (See Exodus 5–12 for the full account.)

It seems strange that Moses has been able to keep his cool under such intense confrontation up to this point. What caused him to lose it finally? I think Scripture gives us a clue: this was going to be the last time Moses was going to stand before Pharaoh. "The LORD said to Moses, 'Yet one plague more I will bring upon Pharaoh and upon Egypt. Afterward he will let you go from here. When he lets you go, he will drive you away completely" (Ex. 11:1).

> OUR SINFUL NATURE ENTICES US TO EXHIBIT EMOTIONS GOD NEVER INTENDED FOR US TO DISPLAY. THE EMOTIONS THEMSELVES AREN'T NECESSARILY WRONG, IT'S WHAT WE DO WITH THEM THAT BECOMES SINFUL.

All the tension Moses had pent up over the course of several months burst in violent emotion. He took his final opportunity to show Pharaoh his true feelings.

I think this passage speaks to another cause for anger in our fear of inadequacy. Look carefully at Exodus 11:3: "And the LORD gave the people favor in the sight of the Egyptians. Moreover, the man Moses was very great in the land of Egypt, in the sight of Pharaoh's servants and in the sight of the people."

That sounds encouraging. But do you notice who never, ever gives Moses props? Pharaoh. Instead he tricks Moses, manipulates him, lies to him, and reneges on his word.

When others doubt our capabilities or diminish our character, our fear of inadequacy triggers a switch within us. Pharaoh's unwillingness to pack up his golf cart and go home at Moses' command hinted to Moses that Pharaoh did not really think Moses could outwit or out-strengthen him.

Our sinful nature entices us to behave independently from God and exhibit emotions that He never intended for us to display. The emotions themselves aren't necessarily wrong, it's what we do with them that becomes sinful. This was a contest between Pharaoh and God. Moses was not expected to be emotionally involved in the battle. He was merely the messenger.

Moses did not need to be the one to win the battle against Pharaoh, God was. He is the only one who softens, molds, and remakes hearts. While the praise of the rest of the people could tempt Moses to demand Pharaoh see him in the same light, Moses needed to stay emotionally detached. Our fear of inadequacy and failure can bring us into battles God never intended us to fight.

Oftentimes these battles surface unexpectedly. Like on hole 8 on a golf course in Petoskey, Michigan. We don't see the confrontation coming and our desire to protect or defend pours out violently.

Anger becomes a distraction that demonstrates our distrust of God. What if we realized our anger is actually the fear that God will not make good on His promises and right every wrong in the end? I'm not suggesting that when a golf ball flies in front of a loved one's face you ought to just shrug your shoulders and move on! But when people bait us into arguments, strike a chord within us that resonates our insecurities, or flip a switch causing a surge of anger to course through our veins, we need to pause and ask, "Is this really my battle to fight?" Maybe this is Operation Confrontation between our enemy and God—and we just happen to be standing on the battlefield.

Shelly loved event planning. A stay-at-home mom, she'd spend a lot of time on decorations, planning menus, baking, and creating Pinterest-worthy designs. One year her son Ben asked for a Lego-themed birthday party. Shelly's mind went whirling with all she could do and began to plan.

About three weeks before Ben's party, he came home from school with an invitation to another boy's party. His friend Jimmy's birthday party would also have a Lego theme. Jimmy's mom, Amy, had four children, did the books for her husband's business, and cared for her father, going to his home to check on him a couple of times each day. Amy didn't have Shelly's event planning skills, or the time for them but, with the help of store-bought goods, provided a fun party for Jimmy.

The following Saturday the same group of boys arrived at Shelly's house for Ben's party. Each boy was greeted with a Lego bag with pieces to build a robot. They walked through a fantastic Lego-constructed maze and decorated the Lego cookies that Shelly had baked. They took Nerf guns and battled it out behind the amazing Lego-constructed barriers in Shelly's backyard. Her Instagram post of the afternoon quickly garnered no less than twenty comments saying how amazing the party looked.

Amy texted her: "Nice party. Jimmy had fun." Shelly gulped. She didn't know how to answer. Should she just say, "Thank you" or "I'm so glad Jimmy could make it," or should she even apologize for throwing the more lavish party with "It's too bad both boys had the same theme"? And before she crafted a reply, anger set in. What was behind Amy's words? Sarcasm? A hidden message that her party was over the top? Was Amy talking with the other moms about how Shelly went crazy with these events and made the rest of them look inadequate? "Nice party"? That's all she could say? Could Amy really be that insecure not to acknowledge Shelly's efforts? Shelly left the text unanswered for hours while she inwardly fumed.

I think Moses kept his cool for fifteen go-arounds because he trusted God. He knew God would prove His strength over Pharaoh. He understood God's purpose in the battle unfolding the way that it did. He could see glimpses of the Israelites' trust being built and the Egyptians' eyes being opened to believe in the power of their God, Yahweh. And when we can see God working, we surrender more easily.

As a mom there are certain things my kids do that get me to spiral out of control quickly. We have strict rules in our home regarding social media usage and online engagement with people we do not know personally. When I find out my kids talk to strangers online, a switch of fear flips on inside of me and I freak out. Why? Because I feel a loss of control, a distrust of strangers who try to talk to my kids, and a general angst regarding all manner of horrific consequences that could come from what my children think is a harmless game they are playing while sitting in a circle of friends.

So, while having social media rules in our home remains wise, mom going off the deep end when the kids make a mistake doesn't exactly open the door for great communication. I can let fear overtake me, or I can trust God to protect my kids when I lack the ability to see everything they are doing on their devices at every moment. Not that I don't religiously check them each night when they turn them in at bedtime! But God *can* see everything at all times. He can guard their heart, soften their heart, and change their heart to want to walk in wisdom. And He loves them even more than Jonathan and I do.

> WE ARE CHOSEN, GIFTED, AND UNCONDITIONALLY LOVED. WHEN WE BELIEVE WHAT GOD HAS ALREADY SAID ABOUT US, WE DON'T BECOME DISTRACTED BY AN ENDLESS SEARCH FOR AFFIRMATION.

I love how Moses never felt the need to defend himself in front of Pharaoh nor demand Pharaoh recognize him as the special chosen deliverer of God. Moses consistently approached Pharaoh with "Godfidence." That's a legit coined word, by the way. It means having faith that God will "act in a right, proper, or effective way."[11] Kind of sounds like God's power and His character again, doesn't it?

Moses never needed Pharaoh's affirmation. When we become angry that others don't recognize our abilities or frustrated that they do not take the time to acknowledge our accomplishments, we have signaled our fear of inadequacy. We want the spotlight on ourselves rather than on God. We want a human to tell us what God already made plain. We are chosen, gifted, and unconditionally loved. When we believe what God has already said about us, we don't become distracted by an endless search for affirmation, nor angry when someone fails to grant it to us. No matter how well-deserved those kudos may be!

Maybe Moses snapped for more noble reasons during this last confrontation with Pharaoh! Thinking of all the suffering the Egyptians have already undergone due to Pharaoh's stubbornness would make just about anybody angry. Now during this last exchange, God would unleash His power to inflict the harshest plague of all. No wonder Moses became angry! He probably echoed my husband's thoughts about the guy on the golf course. "You have no business sitting on this throne, Pharaoh, if you're going to behave so recklessly!"

But most of the time my battles don't involve human life, and hopefully yours do not either.

So why should we allow anger to distract us? Can we trust God to act in a right, proper, or effective way in our relationships and our circumstances? Do we need affirmation from a person when our heavenly Father nods His approval and promises His affection? If someone's inability to see our worth or recognize our accomplishments leaves us reeling in anger, our fear of inadequacy reigns within us.

By the time Amy sent a follow-up text to Shelly—"Ignoring me?"—Shelly had calmed down. She admitted to herself that she had her own set of insecurities, privately defending herself in a battle she needn't have engaged in. She didn't have the outside-the-home responsibilities Amy did. She probably couldn't have handled all that as well as Amy did anyway. And both the Pinterest and store-bought parties were great successes for the kids which, Shelly acknowledged, was the whole point. She quickly returned Amy's text with "Thanks! And Ben had a great time at Jimmy's party."

We lack "Godfidence" when we demand that others affirm our ability to effect ideal outcomes. We basically tell God that it doesn't matter what He thinks about us. Until we find another human to agree with Him and make it clear to us on a daily basis, we just won't believe Him.

Our lack of intimacy with God demands a human substitution. But in our fear of inadequacy we know all too well how incapable we are, so our insecurity generally drives us to self-fulfilling prophesies. And we seek affirmation from people who only bring out the worst in us, leaving us in endless cycles of striving and self-destruction. But we don't see that. Instead we become distracted by our anger toward those who treated us wrongly.

What sparks your anger? Is it distrust in another person? Lack of control over a situation? Angst over an inability to control an outcome? Failure at another person to properly affirm you? Can you choose to handle it with "Godfidence"? God *can* see everything at all times. He can guard your heart. He can protect you from flying golf balls or any other threat, and provide for you. And He loves you more than any human ever could.

# Intentional Trekking

**Bible Reading Plan:**
Exodus 7–11

## Truths for the Journey

- Our anger and frustration actually stem from our fear of inadequacy and failure.

- When we experience a lack of control, a distrust of others, or angst over an outcome, anger and frustration emerge.

- Our emotions aren't necessarily wrong, it's what we do with them that becomes sinful.

- Our fear of inadequacy and failure can bring us into battles God never intended us to fight.

- What if we realized our anger is actually the fear that God will not make good on His promises and right every wrong in the end?

- Godfidence is trusting God to act in a right, proper, or effective way in our relationships and our circumstances.

- Moses consistently approached Pharaoh with Godfidence, allowing God to fight his battles.

- We are chosen, gifted, and unconditionally loved.

## Processing the Journey

1. In what circumstances or situations do you struggle with anger?

2. Do you tend to let your emotions erupt or do you tend to stuff them down?

3. What is your favorite sport? Do you like golf? (Okay, that really has nothing to do with the subject of this book! I am just curious!)

4. What is an area of your life in which you need more Godfidence? Does your struggle come more from an imperception of God's power or from a lack of intimacy with His character?

5. Do you have someone in your life who affirms you? Who is it and how do they do it?

6. Read 1 Thessalonians 5:9–15. In what ways does Paul emphasize encouragement or affirmation in this passage?

7. Who in your life needs affirmation? How could you provide it for them and remind them of their identity as God's chosen child and speak over them the beautiful ways you see God has gifted them?

## Passionate Prayer

*Dear Jesus, give me Godfidence: the ability to trust You to act in a right, proper, or effective way in my relationships and my circumstances. Show me where I am not believing in Your great capability or Your goodness of character. Draw me more intimately into You so I can rest in the fullness of who You are.*

## CHAPTER NINE

# The Quickest or the Safest

*But God led the people around by the way*
*of the wilderness toward the Red Sea.*

Exodus 13:18

When Jennifer's son Brady was diagnosed with special needs, her nightstand turned into a bookstore. She read everything she could find to try to help her son, marching defiantly toward solutions. She studied diet plans, exercise routines, social interaction ideas, the latest treatments, and the best schools. If there was something about helping a child with Brady's needs, Jennifer read it. She took Brady to doctors across the country for testing. She became an expert on educational laws for children with disabilities. Jennifer devoured every single resource available to her.

Some changes in Brady's diet seemed to make a difference. Certain routines lessened his outbursts. Jennifer created a program so that Brady could go to church, preschool, and even a music class in their local community, conquering his exclusion from normal childhood activities. She became an advocate for other moms with children like Brady, becoming a known local expert in the field. But one thing

Jennifer could not do was cure Brady. Despite all the knowledge she gained, she could not heal Brady's mind.

Sometimes the route God chooses seems laborious, circular, or full of so many stops and detours we forget where we are going. When we cannot clearly see ourselves moving forward, a fear of inadequacy sets in and we tend to strive harder so we can pinpoint some sort of tangible progress in our lives. The Israelites needed to wait several long months before God finished the plagues on Pharaoh, revealing Himself to both the Israelites and the Egyptians. Throughout this process, no new freedom came. The repeated answer from God, "You will see what I will do!" More waiting. God's people remained slaves in Egypt.

Now, deliverance has come! The Israelites have finally left Egypt! Take a look at God's travel plans:

> When Pharaoh let the people go, God did not lead them by way of the land of the Philistines, although that was near. For God said, "Lest the people change their minds when they see war and return to Egypt." But God led the people around by the way of the wilderness toward the Red Sea. And the people of Israel went up out of the land of Egypt equipped for battle.— Exodus 13:17–18

The Lord knows whether to test our patience or our courage. It appears that while this route might not have been the quickest, it was probably the safest. God knows from which difficulties we need the greatest protection. He knows the condition of our hearts even more than we do—the areas where we will readily trust and obey and the parts of us that are still unwilling. The Israelites may have been armed for battle, but they were not yet ready to fight! When God takes us on an indirect path, we need to trust His discretion.

There was another battle the people of Israel had to fight. A battle of trust. And God actually orchestrates Israel's travels so that they become hemmed in on every side with the Egyptians in hot pursuit.

Look at what God does next:

> Then the LORD said to Moses, "Tell the people of Israel to turn
> back and encamp in front of Pi-hahiroth, between Migdol and
> the sea, in front of Baal-zephon; you shall encamp facing it,
> by the sea. For Pharaoh will say of the people of Israel, 'They
> are wandering in the land; the wilderness has shut them in.'"—
> Exodus 14:1-3

Consider this description of their path. "Backtrack, retrace
all the steps you just took, all the way up to Baal Zephon . . . they
stood at the waters of the Red Sea. To the north were strong enemy
fortresses. To the south, blazing deserts. To the west, Egypt itself.
They were boxed in. There was no back door—a geographical trap
with no possibility of escape."[12] And Pharaoh and his army are on
their way, racing toward them on their swift chariots.

Has God ever asked you to turn back? Perhaps you felt like you
were moving forward in your spiritual, emotional, or personal life
and suddenly you seemed to be wandering around in circles or
heading backward. That can be a very frustrating and defeating
experience, can't it? Like the perfect scenario for snarls of suggested
failure to start sounding off in our heads. Cue the mind's racing plans
to strive forward, despite God closing every door.

I've been there. I found myself finally gaining ground in a
particular relationship that, well frankly, always seemed to bring
out the worst in me. I felt like I was beginning to make peace with
our differences and learning to extend grace rather than criticism.
Then bam! The right set of circumstances erupted, propelling me
back to square one, baffled by how much ground gained with such
hard work could suddenly be lost so quickly. In those moments, we
wonder why God allows such things. In my own life, God has used
those times of defeat to show me several things:

- He reminded me of His power, deliverance and sovereignty
  and my desperate need for Him.

- He reminded me from just how deep of a pit He once pulled me! If I continue to justify my rebellion in refusing to offer grace to another, there is a very real possibility that I will end up back in that very same pit. An inability to offer grace to others is the first sign that we remain unable to accept grace for ourselves.

- He allowed me to catch a glimpse of just how far He had brought me when I chose to follow Him in obedience rather than continuing to forge my own paths.

- He has asked me to go back and minister to those who are still there.

Do any of those resonate with you? One universal thread weaves through all of the above scenarios: Exodus 14:4 says, "I will get glory over Pharaoh and all his host, and the Egyptians shall know that I am the LORD." One thing Jennifer could do in her wrestling over her inability to cure Brady was share her faith. As she spoke with school personnel, other mothers with special needs children, and medical professionals, she implored them to understand that her strength in advocating and understanding her son came from God. Her fight was rooted in faith in a good God. She brought glory to Him even in her doubts and questioning.

> SOMETIMES GOD MAY CALL US TO RETRACE OUR STEPS, AND OTHER TIMES HE MAY CALL US TO GO BACK AND FACE OUR ENEMY.

God will not waste this return trip, of that we can be sure. But God was not merely asking the Israelites to backtrack to build trust, He also created a scenario to defeat their enemy completely. Look carefully at what God was doing. "And the LORD hardened the heart of Pharaoh king of Egypt, and he pursued the people of Israel while the people of Israel *were going out defiantly*" (Ex.14:8).

Suddenly, however, the Israelites have a change of heart. "When Pharaoh drew near, the people of Israel lifted up their eyes, and behold, the Egyptians were marching after them, and they *feared greatly. And the people of Israel cried out to the LORD"* (Ex. 14:10).

Not so bold now, are we? Sometimes God may call us to retrace our steps, and other times He may call us to go back and face our enemy. The Israelites had been marching "out defiantly" but now they were quaking in fear. The command most often given in Scripture is "Do not fear" or "Do not be afraid." When God forces us to face our enemy, He is gaining glory for Himself by showing us a dramatic display of His power and deliverance, working to drive out fear once and for all. Up until the thunderous roar of the Egyptian chariots, I would dare bet the Israelites did not even entertain the possibility that they had any fear of the Egyptians. But when God put them in the right circumstances, their courage vanished.

WHEN GOD PUTS US IN A PLACE WHERE OUR ONLY HOPE IS HIM, WE HAVE NO CHOICE BUT TO LAY DOWN OUR FEAR OF INADEQUACY AND EMBRACE GOD'S SUFFICIENCY.

God desires to rid us of our fear. He wants us to trust implicitly in His deliverance and protection. He will even use our fear to gain glory for Himself by defeating those things of which we are afraid. When an attack comes into your life, look for God to gain glory for Himself through it. And look for fear to be vanquished.

But in this immediate moment, surrounded on all sides, there is no deliverance in sight. All striving ceased. They remained boxed in with nowhere to go and nothing to do. The people began to do what we naturally default toward when our deliverance doesn't come in our timeline. *They started looking for someone to blame.*

And Moses' leadership skills are critically questioned. We see Moses' habit of crying out to God for direction displayed here again. As soon as the self-doubt set in, Moses cried out to God.

When God puts us in a place where our only hope is Him, we have no choice but to lay down our fear of inadequacy and embrace God's sufficiency. We don't have what it takes and we know it. We stop trying so hard and rely fully on God for the outcome, realizing He is the only one adequate to secure a good one.

Jennifer had gone everywhere she could for answers for Brady and had absorbed every bit of knowledge she found, but still knew that her journey of discovery was incomplete. When she got to the point where she knew more about Brady's condition than his pediatrician, physical therapist, speech pathologist, and preschool teacher, she cracked. There was nothing left to learn. Nothing new to try. No secret treasure to uncover to heal Brady. And she fell into a deep depression. All that knowledge unearthed revealed nothing but dust, choking the life out of Jennifer.

Several months after coming to the end of her quest for knowledge in how to help Brady, this desperate mom cried out to God in her brokenness. She felt so helpless and so afraid. How would Brady function as he got older? Would he have friends? Who would take care of him when Jennifer and her husband were no longer able? What did the future hold for him?

And even though God did not immediately answer all those questions for her, Jennifer felt a peace she had not known before her surrender, a peace that carried her through the years of raising her precious son. She could not cure Brady. She could not fully control his future. She had no choice but to come to the end of herself and place Brady in God's hands. While she did not know the "hows," she somehow sensed in her heart that God would be enough and would make a way for her son.

> IN AND OF OURSELVES WE ARE COMPLETELY INADEQUATE, BUT I AM IS ENOUGH. WHERE WE END, HE BEGINS. WILL WE ALLOW GOD TO REMIND US THAT HE IS THE GOD OF THE IMPOSSIBLE?

As Moses comes to the end of himself, what does God tell him to do? Start leading! Once we cease striving and embrace surrender, God begins to show us His plans. He gives Moses specific directions on how to direct the people. God created circumstances to authenticate His ability to guide them to safety, while at the same time revealing His glory both to Moses and the people. While it appears that Moses did not quite know all of the "hows," he trusted God would take care of His people.

> And Moses said to the people, "Fear not, stand firm, and see the salvation of the LORD, which he will work for you today. For the Egyptians whom you see today, you shall never see again. The LORD will fight for you, and you have only to be silent."—Exodus 14:13–14

Whenever we are waiting on God to work something out on our behalf, one underlying question races through our minds: *What should I do?*

We stand firm refusing to give in to fear. Because when God backs us up into a corner, tells us to stand firm and wait for Him to work out His salvation on our behalf, He's got a plan for deliverance in mind. A plan beyond our wildest imagination. A plan so big and so amazing, only He could concoct it. And the results will be miraculous. All we have to do is stand still and wait. But He doesn't deliver us just so He can do a miracle. He delivers us and destroys the plan of our enemy. He builds our trust in Him and invites us to give Him all the glory.

It's so often God's way to pen us in so He can unexpectedly provide a way out . . . usually one we never saw coming, and we give Him the glory for His timely intervention. We know it wasn't us. And when others witness God working on our behalf, they take notice, especially when we are following God's orders on resolute trust that He will keep His promises to us. When we are in a season of life where we feel stuck and hopeless, these are the exact circumstances for God to work because there's nothing more we ourselves can do. In and of ourselves we are completely inadequate, but I AM is enough. Where we end, He begins. Will we allow God to remind us that He is the God of the impossible?

Moses had no idea how God was going to rescue Israel in this moment, but he was confident that God would. Moses never would have imagined something like parting the Red Sea!

When God brings us back to square one, wandering around in circles, or backed into a corner, He is bringing us to the end of ourselves. Friend, I don't know what route you are on today with Jesus. I don't know if He has you on a road that feels like it's going nowhere, at a dead standstill, or penned in on all sides with no way out. But this I do know: He has you on that path for a reason. He has a purpose taking you down this particular path at this precise time. And no matter how rocky the road, I also know this: it is a path of restoration and redemption.

So, venture on!

# *Intentional Trekking*

## Bible Reading Plan:
Exodus 13–14

## Truths for the Journey

- God knows the why behind the roundabout wait.

- God knows from which difficulties we need the greatest protection.

- An inability to offer grace to others is the first sign that we remain unable to accept grace for ourselves.

- God does not have us backtrack just to build trust; He also works to defeat our enemy completely.

- God desires to rid us of our fears. He wants us to trust implicitly in His deliverance and protection.

- When God puts us in a place where our only hope is Him, we finally lay down our fear of inadequacy and embrace God's sufficiency.

- Once we cease striving and embrace surrender, God begins to show us His plans.

## Processing the Journey

1. When has God ever made you wait? What did you learn in the process? Were you able to look back and see the why?

2. Which area of your life is currently undergoing a greater test: your patience or your courage? How so?

3. Do you have a person in your life with whom you struggle to extend grace? What makes it so difficult?

4. Has God ever placed you in a position that revealed a hidden fear you did not know you had? Why do you think God orchestrates our circumstances specifically to rid us of our fears?

5. In our fear of inadequacy one strategy we implement to try to overcome is to become an expert regarding our situation, like Jennifer's example. Why will knowledge alone regarding a circumstance not be enough to change it?

6. What is a situation you are currently facing in which you're waiting to see the salvation of the Lord?

## Passionate Prayer

*Dear Jesus, help me see where I am trying to take matters into my own hands by relying on worldly knowledge instead of Your wisdom. Help me trust that You are orchestrating my circumstances in order to uncover my fear. Help me trust that You will be enough when I can't see all the "hows." Help me surrender the route to Your perfect path You have for me.*

## CHAPTER TEN

# *Juggling Jealousy*

*And they said, "Has the L*ORD *indeed spoken only through Moses?*
*Has he not spoken through us also?" And the L*ORD *heard it.*
*Numbers 12:2*

I hung up the phone, relieved to end the conversation. Her disappointment that we couldn't get together devastated me. *Who knew I could be any more devastated than I already was?* I mused bitterly. My friend was only in town for a couple of days and wanted me to meet her new baby girl. We had made plans. But I cancelled at the very last minute, feigning a cold and concern for the baby. I didn't have it in me to gush over her darling blue-eyed girl while my own aching belly remained empty of life.

I wanted to rejoice with her. I knew how many years she had waited to be gifted with motherhood. Her miracle story brought hope to my own heartbreak. But the jealousy burned equally brightly. I had to cancel meeting with her. I plodded out to the kitchen to pour another cup of coffee. As I yanked the pitcher out in frustration, the Lord pierced my heart. "If you never birth a child will you pull away from everyone who does?" It seemed with each passing month I had fewer and fewer friends still waiting for motherhood. The birth announcements flooded my email and mailbox. "What am I supposed to do, Lord? I want to be happy for them . . . I *am* happy for them. But the pain remains unbearable just like my belly. Unbearable. Unable to bear a child. Infertile. Dark and empty."

No other emotion sardonically salutes our fear of inadequacy like jealousy. Not only can we not secure the outcome we want, we cannot satiate our destructive emotions either. We withdraw and isolate, trying to protect ourselves from the pain. Or we pour ourselves into countless pursuits, somehow striving toward significance salving our scars of hurt and disappointment.

Shannon, Cassie, and Liz frequently went to networking luncheons together. They each were part of a home-based sales business and swapped promotional ideas, product knowledge, and sales strategies. They also understood the ever-shifting work/home balance while trying to make some extra income for their family. They felt grateful to have each other on the journey because they each sensed that the others understood their goals, motivation, and life's struggles. But then Cassie's business made an unexpected breakthrough and she signed a contract with a local shop owner in their town. Cassie's sales soared and Shannon and Liz struggled with jealousy.

> WE HANG UP ON THE RELATIONSHIP FEIGNING A HEAD COLD, WHEN IN ACTUALITY IT'S OUR ICY HEART THAT'S BEEN CRUSHED AND SHATTERED.

Cassie frequently began to receive text messages from them letting her know they were leaving her out. "Hi Cassie, Shannon and I are driving together to the November luncheon. I have to drop my car off at the dealership for maintenance and she agreed to follow me and then take me to the luncheon afterward, so we'll see you there."

Then when Cassie earned a big reward from the parent company, her first thought was to share it with her friends who knew firsthand how hard she'd had to work to earn it. The company always made a big "to do" over these awards and Cassie hoped her friends would take her shopping for something new to wear. When she texted them the news, she got this reply: "Hi Cassie, Liz and I decided not to go to the annual conference this year. Neither of us can swing it financially. I guess you'll have to go alone. Sorry."

Nothing shoves our fear of inadequacy in our face like watching others succeed. It's like a flashing arrow points down on them that says, "Winner!" and when we look in the mirror all we see is a giant L for Loser on our own forehead. We cite their success as proof positive that they have something we lack. Sometimes we look at them and think, "What do they have that I don't? Why can't I figure out what's wrong with me?" In order to protect ourselves from these debilitating emotions, we disassociate from them. We may not even intend to be unkind or make them feel rejected, we just default into self-protection and try and flee from our dangerous emotions. We hang up on the relationship feigning a head cold, when in actuality it's our icy heart that's been crushed and shattered.

About thirty days after the exodus from Egypt, Miriam and Aaron become bitten by the bug of jealousy. God brings about a mighty deliverance and then follows it by the wonder of water from the rock, then the miracle of manna and quail. Right after the Red Sea miracle, we see Miriam take a position of leadership, leading the women in song in Exodus 15:20–21.

It seems Miriam had always been a quick thinker. Even as a young child, when her mother put Moses in the basket in the Nile, it had been Miriam who bravely approached the Egyptian princess suggesting she hire her own mother to nurse baby Moses (see Exodus 2). Miriam is a brave, no-nonsense firstborn, who thinks on her feet and takes charge, expecting to be heard.

But since the Red Sea event, when Miriam had led the people in song, she suddenly seems silent in the account. We don't hear a peep from her. Until now. She wants to know why Moses is always the one in charge and it appears she goes to Aaron with her question. "Has the LORD indeed spoken only through Moses? Has he not spoken through us also?" (Num. 12:2). Let me paraphrase: *What does Moses have that we don't?*

God answers that question for Miriam and, indirectly, for Aaron. "Hear my words: If there is a prophet among you, I the LORD make myself known to him in a vision; I speak with him in a dream. Not so with my servant Moses. *He is faithful in all my house.* With him I speak mouth to mouth, clearly, and not in riddles" (Num. 12:6–8a). I hope you noticed what Moses had. *Character.* God did not exalt Moses due to his unique capabilities; He embraced him because of his character. Moses was faithful.

When our fear of inadequacy sets us into striving mode trying to gain new skills, greater knowledge, a wider networking arena, or a clever strategy to ensure success, we ought to pause and take a look in the mirror. When it comes to our character, do we have a flashing arrow that says, "Winner!" or a giant L on our forehead because we've neglected what matters most? *Faithfulness.*

D. L. Moody has been widely quoted as observing, "Our greatest fear should not be of failure, but of succeeding at something that doesn't really matter." No one will ever outshine our faithfulness. We all ought to strive to hear the words of Jesus, "Well done, good and *faithful* servant!"

But notice how Miriam began this jealous rant. She questioned Moses' character. "Miriam and Aaron spoke against Moses because of the Cushite woman he had married" (Num. 12:1). Scholars vary on whether this woman refers to his wife Zipporah or a subsequent marriage, but regardless, Miriam poses a concern over Moses' choices, as the Israelite men were not to marry foreign women who worshiped false gods. Notice nothing about the woman's character is mentioned at all, and Miriam may have seen her as a possible rival in her current leadership position. Miriam enjoyed being the most influential woman in Israel as Moses' sister.

God heard Miriam's complaining and immediately confronted her. His admonition is to all of us when we question others' successes:

"Why then were you not afraid to speak against my servant Moses?" (Num. 12:8). God makes it clear to Miriam, who appears to be the instigator in this confrontation, that her behavior angers Him. He punishes her with leprosy. A bite from the jealousy bug will always lead to death if left untreated.

Moses, in great humility, intercedes for her and God heals Miriam's leprosy. But God still sends her out of the camp in shame for seven days. And Israel stays stuck in their campsite waiting to move on until her punishment is over. Though Miriam's jealousy was dealt with, it still had consequences for others. We are foolish to think we can foster jealousy in our heart and it remain unnoticed. Eventually it will surface. Jealousy reveals our fear of inadequacy and the lie that God withholds good things from us. God longs to grow our faithfulness before He fosters our success.

> JEALOUSY REVEALS OUR FEAR OF INADEQUACY AND THE LIE THAT GOD WITHHOLDS GOOD THINGS FROM US. GOD LONGS TO GROW OUR FAITHFULNESS BEFORE HE FOSTERS OUR SUCCESS.

Instead of striving so hard to achieve what we desire, we ought to surrender our dreams to God, asking Him to build His faithfulness within us. When we trust God to grant us the good things He has planned for us when our character is ready to handle it, we focus on what He is doing *within us* rather than what He is doing *through others*.

Sarah worked so hard to meet her weight loss goals. Her doctor had talked to her about her need to take better care of herself, so when her son's wedding was added to the calendar, Sarah got to work. Nothing like five hundred wedding photos for motivation. Sarah knew she'd never be a marathon runner, but she and her sister scheduled morning walks four days a week before Sarah went to work. And the pounds started to drop.

Sarah felt great, and within two months she had gone down two dress sizes. She also gave up her favorite fast food restaurant for a while, trying to eat more fruit and vegetables besides French fries. (Yes, potatoes are vegetables. Do not argue with me on this!)

By the end of the second month, she posted a photo on Instagram celebrating her success. Many people congratulated her on her perseverance and Sarah felt proud of herself.

Later that afternoon, when her workday was over, she reopened her Instagram to respond to some additional congratulatory messages. Her best friend from high school, Jenna, flashed across her phone with her size 2 muscular body bearing a barbell. Sarah's heart sank. She suddenly felt like a frumpy, middle-aged woman whose days of fit and pretty were long gone. "Why bother?" she asked herself, resigned. "I am never going to look toned and trim." And before Sarah knew it she found herself in the drive-thru at the fast food restaurant.

Our fear of inadequacy tells us that if we aren't the best at something, then we aren't good at it at all. Sarah did not need to become a body builder; she needed to become healthy and feel good about her perseverance, her increased energy, and better sleep patterns. But jealousy tells us to relentlessly strive and scheme even if it kills us, or to simply quit altogether. Neither extreme embodies faithfulness.

Sometimes we can be on the opposite end, however. Those whom we thought we could count on don't come through. What do we do when those who are supposed to support us oppose us? It's the betrayal of those closest to us that bites the hardest. And why wouldn't it? Doesn't it make sense that those who know us best ought to be the first to recognize our inadequacy?

Moses faced the blame and the rejection of the people of Israel countless times. Now his own brother and sister betray him because they're jealous he is God's chosen leader. Miriam doesn't see any of the burden, she only sees the benefits—her brother's the one in power, the problem solver, and the deliverer. The guy on the stage. She doesn't feel the weight of the burden.

This had to hurt Moses. His own brother and sister! Rejection from our own flesh and blood is brutal. If we can't count on them, who can we count on? Yet God shows Moses that even in their jealousy and cattiness, God would prove to be Moses' friend and come to his aid. Just as He will come to ours when we run to Him.

As we take strides in overcoming our fear of inadequacy, we encounter others who have been bitten by the bug of jealousy or consumed by their own previous scars. They will rip open our old wounds and invite us to nurse our fears. God teaches us that He will be enough when others disappoint us. Sometimes we become bitten ourselves and as we sit alone in shame we need to trust that God can and will restore us as we wait for Him. It took lots of tears to overcome my jealousy. My body never did bear life but my heart overflowed through adoption of our beautiful children. God grew our family by His bounty instead of biology. (And you moms who went through labor can keep your agonizing birth stories—I walked out of the hospital feeling like a million bucks each time!)

Who doesn't love having people in our life to celebrate our successes? I still feel ashamed over not celebrating my friend's little girl that day. Of course, we all long for people to rejoice with us. It's what drove Sarah and Jenna to post their photos on Instagram. Other people speaking life into us temporarily drowns out the lies of inadequacy that replay through our mind: *I am a failure.* But only God holds the power to rewrite our emotional script. He alone can change the sentence from "failure" to faithful.

*He is faithful in all my house.*

But let's look at God's question to Miriam and Aaron again more closely: *Why then were you not afraid to speak against my servant Moses?* This includes our self-talk too. Not just what others say about us. It's the same question we ought to ask when we speak negatively about ourselves.

Do we trust God to be enough? To make us faithful so we neither strive ourselves to exhaustion nor lazily quit? And when others become jealous over the work God is doing within us and then through us, will we trust God to confront their jealousy on our behalf?

By the way, Cassie went to her annual conference, received her reward, and celebrated that evening on a dinner cruise with her husband. Her Bible study friends brought her a cupcake and a balloon. And her sister posted on Facebook how incredibly proud she was of Cassie. Not everyone will be happy for our success. Our fear of inadequacy and jealousy will make it a struggle to always celebrate others. But our God, who is *faithful*, will teach and transform us *toward faithfulness*. And when we become bitten by the bug of jealousy or suffer the sting of its poison through others' rejection, God will be enough to get us through. It's not success we are after in the end: it's faithfulness.

"Success is not final, failure is not fatal: it is the courage to continue that counts."[13]

# Intentional Trekking

## Bible Reading Plan:
Numbers 12

## Truths for the Journey

- Nothing shoves our fear of inadequacy in our face like watching others succeed.

- God did not exalt Moses due to his unique capabilities; He embraced him because of his character.

- "Our greatest fear should not be of failure, but of succeeding at something that doesn't really matter."[14]

- A bite from the jealousy bug will always lead to death if left untreated.

- Jealousy reveals our fear of inadequacy and the lie that God withholds good things from us.

- God longs to grow our faithfulness before He fosters our success.

- God will be enough when others disappoint or betray us.

## Processing the Journey

1. Have you ever found yourself on the outside of your tribe like Cassie? How did God meet you there?

2. Under what circumstances do you tend to look in the mirror and see a giant L on your forehead?

3. Why do you think God values faithfulness over success?

4. Have you ever been tempted to quit a goal you were pursuing? What caused you to want to give up?

5. Why is it so hard to focus on what God is doing within us over what He is doing through others?

6. In what ways do you think social media fosters jealousy or feelings of failure?

7. Have you ever felt let down by someone whom you thought would support you? How did you handle it and how did God come to your aid?

## Passionate Prayer

*Dear Jesus, help me focus on what You are doing in me rather than being consumed with what You are doing through others. Help me turn to You for validation over the affirmation of others. Make me faithful, God, the way You are faithful.*

## CHAPTER ELEVEN

# *Looking at Our Limitations*

*But Moses' hands grew weary, so they took a stone and*
*put it under him, and he sat on it, while Aaron and Hur held up*
*his hands, one on one side, and the other on the other side.*
*So his hands were steady until the going down of the sun.*

*Exodus 17:12*

When we suffer from a fear of inadequacy or failure, allowing other people to see our limitations terrifies us. We want to mask every flaw and foible pretending like we've got it all together. We often assume that if others knew of our limitations, they would outright reject us. We are only accepted when we're perfect.

Perfectionism and micromanaging point to our fear of inadequacy. If we could, we'd work alone where we can control and demand the results we expect at every turn. When we're driven by fear of failure to meet others' expectations, we know we'll work ourselves to death to get it right. Striving serves us well. But inviting others in? That's risky. They may not be as emotionally invested as we are and their standard might be below perfection.

Amanda had been the mastermind behind her church's annual harvest festival for several years. She loved hearing, "Amanda's done it again!" and feeling the satisfaction in knowing she once more had single-handedly pulled off a successful fundraiser, which provided funds to help children go to camp.

Then Holly's family joined the church. Holly, who managed a popular bakery/coffee-house, proposed working with other volunteers to supply fancy dessert baskets as an extra special offering to bolster sales. Despite being urged to accept Holly's idea, Amanda kept putting her off, insisting she had preparations for the entire event well in hand. Plans for the festival went on as usual and, as usual, Amanda worked herself to a frazzle, but this year, she actually became ill with bronchitis and was unable to continue. Several days before the event, there was still much to be done, and Amanda had no choice but to ask for help. She contacted Holly, who agreed to take on the desserts and oversee volunteers for the other details of the festival.

The problem with taking everything on ourselves becomes our inability to pull it off. But God often backs us into a corner with our limited possibilities so He can provide His limitless provision. God brought Moses face to face with his physical limitations. Not long after their departure, an enemy tribe, Amalek, came and attacked the people of Israel, as we read in Exodus 17. Moses summoned Joshua, his second in command, and instructed him to "Choose for us men, and go out and fight with Amalek. Tomorrow I will stand on the top of the hill with the staff of God in my hand" (v. 9).

So that's what Joshua did, and it's quite the interesting story, complete with exciting cinematography. We can picture it: when Moses would hold up his arms, Israel would be winning the battle. But if he grew weary and his arms drooped, then it was Amalek that gained the edge.

Finally Moses' arms became so weary that he could no longer hold them up by himself. His comrades found a large stone for him to sit on, and Aaron held up one of his arms and Hur the other. How did this work out? His hands remained "steady until the going down of the sun" (v. 12). And, led by Joshua, Israel won the battle.

Some scholars suggest that Moses did more than just stand there with his hands in the air. Perhaps God spoke battle strategies to him and Moses communicated to Joshua what to do through giving signals with the staff. This suggests God took a much more active role in the battle and has Moses acting as more of a general, taking orders from his Commander in Chief. But imagine if Moses had refused the help of Aaron and Hur. Amalek most likely would have prevailed and plundered Israel. The defeat may also have incited other nomadic tribes to come and attack Israel later. Israel needed to win that battle, and Moses could not secure their victory alone. He was not physically strong enough. He needed help.

In this battle scene God's honor was also at stake. God's desire was to make Himself known as the One True God, high above all the false gods of the surrounding nations. If Amalek had won, it would mean that God was not powerful enough to defeat Amalek's gods. Look what God instructed Moses to call the altar he built at the conclusion of this battle: "The LORD Is My Banner" (v. 15). That word banner means "rallying-point" or "miracle."[15] When we rally together as brothers and sisters in Christ, our God works miracles on our behalf. How's that for motivation to hand over our fear of inadequacy and invite others in?

Second, God brought Moses face to face with his mental and emotional limitations. Directly after this event, having heard of Israel's victory, Moses' father-in-law Jethro comes to visit Moses in the wilderness, bringing along his wife and two sons. After a wonderful celebration upon his arrival, Moses goes back to work. One of the roles he had taken upon himself was to judge disputes. The process was time-consuming and the long lines of people waiting to see Moses were seemingly endless. Jethro was appalled at the system.

> When Moses' father-in-law saw all that he was doing for the people, he said, "What is this that you are doing for the people? Why do you sit alone, and all the people stand around you from morning till evening?" And Moses said to his father-in-law, "Because the people come to me to inquire of God; when they have a dispute, they come to me and I decide between one person and another, and I make them know the statutes of God and his laws."—Exodus 18:14–16

Whoa! How many applicants would inquire about that employment opportunity? You're the sole guy who communicates with God. You listen to arguments and disputes all day. You have to teach the people everything they are doing wrong and pass judgment on half of them to decide every case. "Sounds like a dream job!" said no one, ever. (Okay, admit it, this could be a summary of motherhood some days! Or is that only my reality?) Please don't forget, there are two million Israelites huddled together in a campsite. Can you imagine the incessant squabbling?

> PART OF RELEASING OUR FEAR OF INADEQUACY IS LEARNING TO BE OKAY WITH OUR LIMITATIONS. NOBODY CAN BE EVERYTHING TO EVERYONE AT ALL TIMES.

But when you have a fear of inadequacy you sign up for the job titled Superman or Wonder Woman, because working alone is your jam. Even when it's awful.

Look at Jethro's sensible response to this scenario. "What you are doing is not good. You and the people with you will certainly wear yourselves out, for the thing is too heavy for you. You are not able to do it alone" (vv. 17–18).

Maybe you need to reread that last sentence, friend. *You are not able to do it alone.* Whatever "it" is in your life. Maybe it's a harvest festival. Or a book fair. Or a sick family member. A financial setback requiring you to work more hours or return to work full-time. A dysfunctional marriage. Single parenting. An addiction. A prodigal child. *You will certainly wear yourself out.* Even Wonder Woman went home to Themyscira to seek advice sometimes.

Isn't it interesting that God taught Moses these lessons back to back in the Exodus account? If Moses was anything like me, I'd need more than one admonition from God regarding the importance of asking for help. Part of releasing our fear of inadequacy is learning to be okay with our limitations. Nobody can be everything to everyone at all times. We have to learn to accept this and set realistic expectations of ourselves. Perfection becomes a prison if we don't relinquish unhealthy ideas about performance.

We also need to be free to encourage others to lead in the ways they are gifted. Moses falsely assumed he was the only one who could be trusted to settle disputes among the people. Look at Jethro's advice. Delegate. Form committees. Moses, he said, your specialty is this: "You shall represent the people before God . . . and you shall . . . make them know the way in which they must walk and what they must do" (Ex. 18:19–20).

But for lesser disputes, "look for able men from all the people, men who fear God, who are trustworthy and hate a bribe, and place such men over the people as chiefs of thousands, of hundreds, of fifties, and of tens. And let them judge the people at all times" (vv. 21–22a). Sure, Moses would still take care of anything major, but ordinary disputes would be shared with other capable people. Why was this great advice not only for Moses, but for each of us? "So it will be easier for you, and they will bear the burden *with* you" (v. 22b)

Jethro did not tell Moses to do something differently, he just suggested he stop trying to do it all alone. Moses still performed the same tasks, but allowed others to help him. He invited others to bear the burden alongside him. Jethro gave Moses permission to stop performing, breaking him out of the prison of perfectionism.

Look at the outcome: "If you do this, God will direct you, you will be able to endure, and all this people also will go to their place in peace" (v. 23)

When we make peace with our limitations, we find peace in our relationships. We stop believing the lie that everything must be perfect or life will fall apart. We alone cannot be enough to sustain all people at all times in all things. We weren't meant to be. God becomes our rallying point. We gather around Him, inviting Him to be our miracle. Our more than enough.

That year the harvest festival went off without a hitch. Even though Amanda got the flu. And with the addition of Holly's baked goods, they raised an additional several hundred dollars. Amanda, the one-time harvest queen, agreed to expand her royal court for good, adding Holly and others to co-rule her kingdom. And the camp program lived happily ever after.

If God used Amanda's illness, along with teaching Moses *twice* about his limitations, not allowing either of them to go it alone, what do you think He's asking you to place in the hands of someone else for help? I don't have your entrance to the harvest festival covered, but I'll gladly give you a ticket out of Perfection Prison!

Dear friend,

You have permission to stop performing.

# *Intentional Trekking*

## Bible Reading Plan:
Exodus 17:8–15; 18:13–23

## Truths for the Journey

- Perfectionism and micromanaging point to our fear of inadequacy.
- When we rally together as brothers and sisters in Christ, our God works miracles on our behalf.
- Part of releasing our fear of inadequacy is learning to be okay with our limitations.
- Perfection becomes a prison if we don't relinquish unhealthy ideas about performance.
- Jethro gave Moses permission to stop performing, breaking him out of the prison of perfectionism.
- When we make peace with our limitations, we find peace in our relationships.

## Processing the Journey

1. What is a task or responsibility you have a hard time letting go of?

2. Have you ever faced a situation in which you were forced to ask for help? How did you feel and what happened?

3. Why do you think God shows Moses, and subsequently us, Moses' limitations twice in a row in the Exodus narrative?

4. What is something you are facing right now that you know you are unable to do alone? Whom has God placed in your life to help you?

5. Is there a relationship in your life that lacks peace because you are bent on perfection? How would accepting your own limitations or the limitations of others bring peace to this relationship?

## Passionate Prayer

*Dear Jesus, show me where I am trying to control situations. Help me surrender areas of perfectionism over to You. You alone are perfect. Remind me that You desire my heart over my performance. Forgive me when I foolishly try to win Your favor instead of believing You love me regardless and You know my limitations.*

## CHAPTER TWELVE

# Tent Kickers

*Then Moses told his father-in-law all that the LORD had done
to Pharaoh and to the Egyptians for Israel's sake, all the hardship
that had come upon them in the way, and how the LORD
had delivered them. And Jethro rejoiced . . .*

*Exodus 18:8–9*

When my mom began to have psychotic episodes, no one could explain to me why. We went to neurologists, psychiatrists, psychologists, and finally after an appointment at a leading neurological institute we received a diagnosis: Lewy Body Dementia. This horrific disease attacks a person's frontal lobe, leading to drastic personality changes, psychotic episodes, and physical symptoms similar to Parkinson's disease. Needless to say, my mother could not be left alone for even a moment. She hallucinated. She'd stay awake for days on end. She began to lose her balance and fall. She needed twenty-four-hour care, and her behavior remained highly unpredictable.

Her physician at the institute warned that treating Lewy Body sort of equated to a guessing game. We might need to adjust her medications for months before finding a balance that would keep her free from psychoses. In the meantime, we needed to find a place where she could live safely. Over this three-month period I lost ten pounds, broke out in hives, got the flu twice, and barely slept. We desperately needed to find a place for her to live where I knew she would be well cared for and safe. She could not live on her own, and unless we brought in a full-time caregiver, living with us was out of the question. I also battled between keeping her close by and protecting my young children from her erratic behavior.

By God's amazing grace, a brand-new care center opened just two miles from our home. They had a special wing for memory care patients that remained locked and provided full-time supervision for their patients. The grounds were beautiful, and my mom had a corner room overlooking the garden. Even though Lewy Body did not exactly fit with their typical patient population, the director agreed to take her. He loved my mom's sanguine, flamboyant personality, and he took a special interest in her care. I would frequently find my mom dancing in the hallway or singing karaoke in the dining hall. For the first time in months, I saw my always-the-life-of-the-party mom crack a smile. I wept at God's goodness to us.

Once my mom had moved into this care center, all the stress I carried the last four months overtook me like a flood. I slept for three straight days.

Now new stresses awaited. I needed to sell my mom's home to pay for this ritzy place. My mother had always been a meticulous housekeeper, but her last three weeks in her home before we fully understood the full extent of her illness contradicted that fact. A giant stain had set in across her carpet. Clothes were strewn all over her bedroom floor. She burned a hole in her sofa. None of the dishes in her dishwasher had been rinsed and the kitchen smelled horrible. Part of me cringed over allowing anyone to see my mother's home like this. The other part of me knew there was no way I had either the physical or the emotional strength to get this house ready for a realtor to list it.

I felt like a failure allowing others to see my mom's mess. I refused to focus on the facts instead of my feelings. My mother was ill. No one would expect her to care for her home in the same way as a healthy person would. My own health was compromised. I had been sick more than well the last three months. The task was mammoth. My mom had sixty years of stuff crammed in that house—of course I needed help cleaning it out. Those were the facts, but my feelings guilted me into believing I needed to tackle this project solo.

My friends stepped in. "No way, no how, no can do," they insisted. "You have to allow us to help you." Sherry and her husband spent days at my mother's home with me, taking countless trips to the women's shelter with clothing, household items, and small appliances. Danielle and Jen organized my mom's closet and cupboards, selecting and packing clothing to take to her new care home, while delivering the rest to Goodwill. Tami cleaned, loaded, and moved special items to make my mother's new room feel like home. I felt guilty and grateful simultaneously.

WE DON'T WANT TO INVITE OTHERS INTO OUR MESSES OR ADMIT THAT WE CAN'T HANDLE THEM ON OUR OWN. BUT THERE ARE SOME THINGS IN LIFE JUST TOO BIG TO HANDLE ON OUR OWN.

Our fear of inadequacy tempts us to hide. We only want to put our best foot forward, sharing our Instagram-worthy lives. We don't want to invite others into our messes or admit that we can't handle them on our own. Help equals incompetence because we focus on our feelings instead of the facts. There are some things in life just too big to handle on our own.

A tired old adage claims that God won't give us more than we can handle. Guess what? That's not in the Bible or is anything like it. Nowhere does the Bible teach that God won't give us more than we can handle. Some things in life are too big to handle. For me, selling my mom's home was one of them. Sometimes we need God's grace and good friends to get us through.

After months of confronting Pharaoh, accusations from the Israelites about Moses mounted. They claimed that Moses actually intended to kill them rather than deliver them. There were complaints over the lack of water, disappointments over the desert dining experience, and a surprise attack from the Amalekites. Moses needed a three-day nap as well, just like I did. And he needed a good friend. God in His great mercy sends him one. Jethro, his father-in-law, comes and brings Moses' wife and sons along with him. We've learned about the good advice Jethro gave Moses about delegation. Moses also had another powerful breakthrough during Jethro's visit.

**ASKING FOR HELP REQUIRES A DIFFERENT TYPE OF STRENGTH: VULNERABILITY.**

First comes the expected greeting ritual. "Moses went out to meet his father-in-law and bowed down and kissed him. And they asked each other of their welfare and went into the tent" (Ex. 18:7). Then Moses completely unloads onto Jethro the good, the bad, and the ugly. "Then Moses told his father-in-law all that the LORD had done to Pharaoh and the Egyptians for Israel's sake, all the hardship that had come upon them in the way and how the LORD had delivered them" (v. 8). Twice.

Scripture says Moses told Jethro *all* that had happened—*all* the good and *all* the bad.

Notice carefully how Moses words this report: ". . . all that the LORD had done . . . and how the LORD had delivered them." We see Moses emphasizing all that God had done on behalf of His people. Moses clearly realizes it wasn't his endless striving, skills, or abilities, or his adequacy as the chosen leader who brought about these marvels. God did it all. Moses demonstrates great humility here, but he also does something else. While relaying God's wonders on Israel's behalf, he recounts the facts: *this journey had been full of hardship.* Moses focused on the facts. He did not downplay the difficulty the deliverance had demanded of him.

As believers we tend to discount our difficulty. We feel guilty citing our hardships instead of simply being grateful for all God gives us. And truthfully, there are times we can get hyper-focused on hardship. But when we feel like we need to stuff our emotions and cannot ask for help, this shouts shame. Asking for help requires a different type of strength: vulnerability. We believe the lie that we are unworthy to wrestle with disappointment or doubt when things get hard. We think if we are vulnerable with our feelings, others will shake their heads in disapproval. We somehow feel like we are "less than" to admit that at times deliverance demands more than we can deliver and we need help. That doesn't make us ungrateful, it makes us human.

The Bible implies that Jethro came to Moses of his own volition. Moses did not ask him to come. But God knew Moses needed help and sent Jethro at the perfect time. (I'm sure a little time with his wife served Moses well also, but this isn't a marriage book!) And when they arrived, Moses unloaded and invited Jethro into his tent, where he let down his guard and recounted the journey. Without any need for filters—just raw facts and feelings. *This has been hard.*

So much beauty exists in this relationship between Moses and Jethro that we should seek to emulate and attain. We all need people in our lives with whom we can "kick it in our tent"—that is, our own tent kickers. They get us. They know us; the plus, the minus, the whole deal. This is not the person with whom you are real when you are wearing your leader hat. This is not the person with whom you are real when you are wearing your church or ministry hat. This is not even the person with whom you are real when you are wearing your wife, mom, or career hat. This is the person who knows you and gets you when your head is uncovered and you are having your very best hair day or your absolute worst one.

For those of us who are married, our spouse should be one of those people. But truthfully, even after twentysomething years, there are still some female things about me that my husband just does not get, which he will readily admit to you. (Like why I want hair extensions for my birthday, for instance. Or why I need jeans in both light and dark denim. And also why I cannot make a decision, even if my life depended on it, without talking about it out loud for at least fifty-five minutes. Can you relate?) I need godly women who are tent kickers with me, just like my husband needs godly men.

One of the truest tests of a godly tent kicker is that they can delight in your miracles. Jethro rejoiced with Moses over all the good things God had done. When God blesses you with an unexpected gift or opens up the door for an incredible call upon your life, they are delighted for you. They rejoice with you and for you. Your victory is their joy. Jethro made it a point to come and rejoice with Moses, and we do not find a shred of jealousy between them.

These kinds of friendships do not happen overnight. They do not happen because you both like Mexican food—although no one would argue about the bonding power of tacos—or your kids go to school together. These kinds of friendships require work, faithfully exercised over time. For those of us who are married, we understand this completely when it comes to our spouse. But why do we think "happily ever afters" and deep and lasting friendships ought to naturally just evolve if they are meant to be? Marriages fail when not invested in regularly and so do friendships. We have to intentionally build them.

> MOSES AND JETHRO SHARED A LONG HISTORY, WITH DEEP GROOVES OF TRUST CARVED. FOR MANY OF US, WE DEEPLY DESIRE THESE TYPES OF FRIENDSHIPS WITH OTHERS, BUT WE DO NOT WANT TO INTENTIONALLY CARVE OUT THE TIME TO BUILD THEM.

Moses worked for Jethro for forty years. They shared a long history, with deep grooves of trust carved. For many of us, we deeply desire these types of friendships with others, but we do not want to intentionally carve out the time to build them. If we are truly committed to growing in godliness, tent kickers are indispensable.

You know why? Because if there is nobody out there who knows the real you, then there is nobody out there holding you accountable. Or speaking facts over your oftentimes all-encompassing feelings. Not really, anyway. Sure, maybe for a few external behaviors that you are trying to get a handle on, but not with issues of the heart, or your deep fear of not being enough.

Tent kickers know what's really going on inside of you, and they aren't afraid to call you out on it. And you can trust what they are saying is born out of love and your best interest because of their track record.

These tent kickers become powerful partners who can see things we can't, offer fresh perspectives, and transform us with truth. Moses had no idea that he had another forty years to go as Desert Director, and without Jethro calling him out on trying to fulfill all the responsibilities alone, I'm not sure Moses could have endured. It certainly would've been beyond what was humanly possible.

HOW DO WE BEGIN TO BUILD THESE TENT-KICKER TYPES OF RELATIONSHIPS? WHAT ARE SOME THINGS TO LOOK FOR IN PEOPLE THAT WOULD MAKE THEM WORTHY OF BECOMING A TENT KICKER IN OUR LIVES?

If you are hanging out in your tent with no earthly companions, take heart. John 1:14 says, "The Word became flesh and dwelt among us." The word translated "dwelt" implies that Jesus "tabernacled" or resided in a tent among His people. Do you get it? Jesus, the God-man, the eternal, self-existent one, clothed Himself in human flesh and came to earth. Why? So He could become your tent kicker!

I don't care if you feel like you haven't got a friend in the world, you've got a tent kicker and His name is Jesus! He is the most important tent kicker you and I will ever have. He does not want us dwelling in our tents alone with Him all the time though: He wants us to invite some others to join our private party of two.

Notice the results of Moses sharing everything with Jethro. "Now I know that the LORD is greater than all gods" (Ex. 18:11). That is what happens when we finally stoop down from our "I can do this all by myself" pedestals and get honest and real: God becomes exalted. We finally learn to make less of ourselves and much of Him. When we allow people into our lives who can see our imperfections and inadequacies and yet see how intimately and passionately our God still loves us, He becomes magnified. His power, faithfulness, and goodness become more visible.

Let's stop hiding in our tents. We all have messes behind our canvas flaps and you already have got Jesus in there helping you clean it up!

How do we begin to build these tent-kicker types of relationships? What are some things to look for in people that would make them worthy of becoming a tent kicker in our lives? This exchange between Moses and Jethro gives us some great starting points.

You can share both your struggles and your victories.

They delight in your miracles and your successes.

They welcome others into your tent during times of celebrating instead of hoarding your presence.

They will confront you when they see something in your life that "is not good."

They observe and listen, trying to understand your heart before offering their advice.

They give their advice, but then expect you to take it to God before you take action.

They do not get upset when, after seeking God's direction, you decide on a different strategy. (Not a sinful strategy, but an equally noble pursuit!)

Are we one of these people ourselves? Unless we cease striving to look like we have it all together, can manage our lives alone, and never admit to experiencing lack or limitations, we undoubtedly will forfeit these types of friendships. Once we surrender our inadequacies over to Jesus, inviting Him into our tent first, we become free to allow others into our messy dwelling places. We can stand in the doorway demanding everyone believe we only live Instagram-worthy lives or we can open the flap and let others see the real us. Sometimes the most beautiful friendships are born around the messiest tables. And if tacos are being served, well then, even better.

# Intentional Trekking

### Bible Reading Plan:
Exodus 18:1–12

### Truths for the Journey

- There are some things in life just too big to handle on our own.
- Sometimes we need God's grace and good friends to get through.
- When we focus on the facts, we do not downplay the difficulty.
- At times we have to admit that deliverance demands more than we can deliver.
- Asking for help requires a different type of strength: vulnerability.
- One of the truest tests of a godly tent kicker is that they can delight in your miracles.
- These tent kickers become powerful partners who can see things we can't, offer fresh perspectives, and transform us with truth.
- Jesus is the most important tent kicker we will ever have.
- Sometimes the most beautiful friendships are born around the messiest tables.

## Processing the Journey

1. Have you ever faced a circumstance or a situation that was too big to handle on your own?

2. Why does acting like we have everything under control stifle friendship?

3. Have you ever had a tent kicker friend in your life? What made them that kind of friend to you?

4. Do you struggle with asking for help from others? Do you think it's harder to handle life on your own or to be vulnerable and ask for help?

5. Who in your life holds you accountable and speaks the facts, drowning out feelings?

6. What does Jeremiah 17:9 teach us about our heart and our feelings? Why does this make tent-kicker friendships even more important?

7. Who is someone in your life with whom you can intentionally begin to build authentic friendship?

## Passionate Prayer

*Dear Jesus, help me be the same kind of tent kicker You are.
Help me rejoice in others' successes and be willing to speak truth
into others' lives. Remind me of the tremendous vulnerability
You endured leaving the glory of heaven and clothing Yourself in
human flesh. Help me see vulnerability as a strength and a place
of trust in Your sufficiency to fill in the gaps of lack in humanity.
Help me to long for Your presence.*

## CHAPTER THIRTEEN

# Betrayal

*The next day Moses said to the people, "You have sinned*
*a great sin. And now I will go up to the Lord;*
*perhaps I can make atonement for your sin."*

Exodus 32:30

When I began to travel more often to speak at churches and events, my husband and I decided to get our daughter and son each a cellphone. We wanted them to be able to check in with us at any time when they were being cared for by other people or at their friends' houses. We also loved the added security of knowing exactly where they were at all times with the tap of a button on our own media devices. Before handing over the new phone, however, we painstakingly went through all of the "what ifs" and laid out the usage rules. We explained that the phone would be turned in to us each evening and we would check regularly how it had been used throughout the day. If they were not following our rules, we would find out, and there would be consequences.

One evening while reading through Eliana's text threads, we noticed something odd. The conversation did not flow in all of them and there appeared to be gaps. This only happened with one friend in particular and we questioned her about it. She confessed that she had searched online and intentionally deleted some of the texts in the conversation, saying that this person sometimes sent her memes or used language that she knew we wouldn't like. We understood her concern but forbade her from deleting anything further because we wanted to see this person's inappropriate communication. Maybe we needed to help our daughter navigate some friendship boundaries.

After a couple of weeks, it was clear Eliana continued to randomly erase texts from this friend. We instituted random phone checks, taking her phone the minute she got in the car when picking her up after school. It became apparent that Eliana also used inappropriate language at times and the deleted texts were not solely to protect Eliana's friend's reputation, but also her own. Her dishonesty disappointed us ten times more than her word choices in memes (remember my Marine Corps dad?) and we took her phone away for a few weeks.

It broke my heart that our daughter would lie to us. The hardest part was that I honestly thought it inconceivable that she would do so. I had felt bad that she felt caught in the middle between her parents and her friend, when in reality she was covering up her own error. These are hard lessons to learn at thirteen when you want to fit in with your friends at school. And when a mama's trust in her daughter becomes broken, her heart breaks as well. But broken trust also opens opportunities to build trust to new levels. And as Eliana grew older and began to experience ever increasing levels of independence, such as driving and continual internet access to complete her high school assignments, these previous mess-ups provided memories of the importance of setting up personal safeguards and accountability, along with the anguish of broken trust.

In this leg of the journey, Moses faced great disappointment. Moses entrusted Aaron with great responsibility and Aaron failed to act responsibly. This happened when Moses was on Mt. Sinai to receive the Ten Commandments and instructions to build the tabernacle, and he left Aaron in charge.

Moses was a long time returning, and the people grew restless. They wanted a new leader and even new gods. "As for this Moses, the man who brought us up out of the land of Egypt, we do not know what has become of him" (Ex. 32:1b).

Perhaps they forgot what they had promised after a previous trip Moses had taken to Sinai to hear from God: "All that the LORD has spoken we will do" (Ex. 19:8). Now they demanded of Aaron, "Make us gods who shall go before us" (Ex. 32:1a).

"Make us gods"? And incredibly, Aaron concedes to the demand. He instructed the people to donate their gold, melted it down, and "fashioned it with a graving tool and made a golden calf" (v. 4).

Meanwhile up on the mountain, covered by fire and smoke, clearly letting the Israelites know God remained among them, Moses received Aaron's commissioning to become High Priest or Chief Intercessor for the people of Israel. God described in detail Aaron's clothing, his duties, his leadership over the Levites, and the ordained sacrifices in proper worship of the Lord. And what was Aaron doing down below? Leading the people in rebellion against God's law and idol worship. Talk about a contrast! But I am convinced Aaron's foolish acquiescence to the people's command for him to fashion a god to worship was not what upset Moses most. It was his falsehood in relaying what happened.

Look closely:

> And Moses said to Aaron, "What did this people do to you that you have brought such great sin upon them?" And Aaron said, "Let not the anger of my lord burn hot. You know the people, that they are set on evil. For they said to me, 'Make us gods who shall go before us. As for this Moses, the man who brought us up out of the land of Egypt, we do not know what has become of him.' So I said to them, 'Let any who have gold take it off.' So they gave it to me, and I threw it into the fire, and out came this calf."—Exodus 32:21–24

I hope you noticed what Moses attempted to do with his question. And what he desperately hoped to be the case behind these circumstances. Moses wanted to believe that Aaron had made this decision under great distress and derision. He hoped Aaron might prove innocent in this mess and only unable to stop it. It's painful enough when someone doesn't come through and disappoints us, but even worse when it seems that they did so easily and willingly.

Look at Aaron's response. He caught on to Moses' desire to find him innocent and he piggy-backed on this suggestion. *These people are wicked, Moses, you know that.* He shifted blame but first coated Moses' bleeding heart with flattery calling him "my lord."

Then Aaron shifted the blame even further. *You were gone a long time, Moses. You left me alone with them for way too long!* That's a sneaky way to suggest this whole ordeal was actually Moses' fault. But then the most devastating part occurs. Aaron lied to Moses' face. Aaron came up with a plan, asked the people for gold, and fashioned the calf in the fire with his very own hands. "Out came this calf" indeed! But that's not the story he told to Moses at all. Talk about betrayal!

I'll never forget the way my friend Melissa sobbed as she recounted her story, stopping countless times to weep, while I sat there dumbfounded.

Jim began to stay later and later at the office. Melissa knew in her heart something was up. On the one hand she relished his absence because every time he was home they argued heatedly or she shivered under his icy silence and cold shoulder. One morning while Melissa grew teary on her patio over her cup of coffee, her neighbor Tina noticed. She came over and sat down, asking her what was the matter. Melissa broke. Tina patiently sat and listened as Melissa confided and cried. Later that afternoon Melissa sent her a text that simply said, "Thanks for listening. Please don't tell anyone."

"Anytime. Your secret's safe with me."

Tina kept her promise, and when the two crossed paths, she never even hinted about Melissa's teary confession that day a few months before.

Jim seemed to travel even more and with his increased absence the opportunity for arguing lessened. The truce was peaceful, but Melissa knew Jim's heart was no longer at home and she wondered who had captured it.

One day Melissa was surprised to see a "For Sale" sign in front of Tina's house. She went over and knocked on the door. Tina's husband, Mike, answered.

"I had no idea you were moving!" Melissa told him. "We are going to miss you guys," she said with a friendly smile.

Mike didn't smile back. "You honestly don't know, do you?" he stammered.

"Know what?" whispered Melissa with a sick feeling stirring in her stomach.

"Our spouses are having an affair!" he snapped. Melissa stumbled two steps backward and then turned and ran into her house, raced upstairs, and collapsed on her bed, sobbing uncontrollably.

"I *knew* he was in love with someone else," she wailed. "But Tina?! The very person I trusted with my pain!"

Melissa shook with anger and dropped back onto her pillow in grief. She vacillated so violently between longing for Jim to love her again and fury toward him for betraying her, she felt her heart shred into a thousand pieces.

In the midst of Aaron's betrayal, Moses faced a tremendous test. Two tests actually. Would his pride seep in, taking him beyond justifiable anger to utter vengeance, or would he humbly run to God for help in this devastation? Take a look at God's offer to Moses for vengeance.

> And the LORD said to Moses, "Go down, for *your people*, whom *you brought up out of the land of Egypt*, have corrupted themselves. They have turned aside quickly out of the way that I commanded them. . . . Now therefore let me alone, that my wrath may burn hot against them and I may consume them, in order that I may make a great nation of you."—Exodus 32:7–8, 10

God offered Moses a pass to choose vengeance over forgiveness. He tested Moses' heart. God implied that it was Moses who delivered and led the people out of Egypt. With all the grumbling Moses has thus far endured it would be tempting to take some credit for his hard work and tough obedience. But instead he demonstrated his deep dependence on God. Moses insisted that God Himself was the deliverer and the leader. Look at Moses' response to God's suggestion, "But Moses implored the LORD his God and said, 'O LORD, why does your wrath burn hot against *your* people, whom *you* have brought out of the land of Egypt with great power and with a mighty hand?'" (Ex. 32:11).

> GOD TESTED MOSES' HEART TO SEE IF HE MIGHT REMAIN HUMBLE BEFORE GOD, AND HE PASSED WITH FLYING COLORS.

Moses gets an A+ here in godliness in my book. He recounted to God his simple role in all of this: *I'm just the messenger, God. It was Your power and mighty hand that set us free!* In the middle of devastation our pride tempts us to color ourselves in the best light and paint our betrayer in the worst one. God tested Moses' heart to see if he might remain humble before God, and he passed with flying colors.

Second, when God threatened to severely punish the people for their rebellion and destroy them completely, how easy it would have been for Moses to agree with God about this idea of revenge. The Israelites have railed and rallied against Moses and his leadership from day one. To just be done with this assignment would be a relief! But Moses does something entirely unexpected: he interceded for the people.

> "Turn from your burning anger and relent from this disaster against your people. Remember Abraham, Isaac, and Israel, your servants, to whom you swore by your own self, and said to them, 'I will multiply your offspring as the stars of heaven, and all this land that I have promised I will give to your offspring,

and they shall inherit it forever.' And the LORD relented from the disaster that he had spoken of bringing on his people."— Exodus 32:12b–14

What?! I'm not sure I could pass this test. In my inadequacy it would be pretty easy to hand over all the accomplishments to God. I know how utterly incapable I am to deliver anyone, including myself. But intercede for the very people who criticized and betrayed me? Whoa! That would take a miracle!

We may not face a situation as devastating as Melissa did when her husband and friend both betrayed her, but we will face these same kinds of tests in life. People will fail us and lie to us, and we'll be tempted to desire vengeance from having to bear the brunt of their poor choices. Maybe it's the parent who walked out. Maybe it's the coworker who did not follow through on the project and lied to the boss, blaming us for their failure. Maybe it's the teacher who promised to help our struggling child but didn't. Maybe it's the friend who didn't show up in that moment we needed them most. Maybe it's the pastor who didn't confront our spouse in their sin. We will feel betrayed.

In our conquest to defeat our fear of inadequacy we can become tempted toward self-sufficiency. We'll pull back and isolate, and decide that being alone is the only way to protect ourselves. Moses could have nursed his wounds thinking, "After all I've done for these people? All the time, sacrifices, criticism I've endured and loyalty I've displayed, and this is how they treat me!" Or we'll be tempted to quit leading, cease loving, and walk away, asking God to take us somewhere else with someone else and start over. And our deep fear of inadequacy—of not being enough—will tempt us to believe that they failed us because we weren't good enough to deserve loyalty, honesty, or love.

Moses turned away from both temptations. He acknowledged God's sovereignty in their deliverance and His faithfulness to His promises. He turned to God and reminded himself, along with

God, about the character and the capability of the God he served. (Not that God needed reminding, but Moses needed to decide if he would turn toward self-sufficiency and striving or would surrender in the wake of this devastation.)

What will we do in those moments? Will we turn to God for direction? Will we humbly acknowledge that He is in charge even when everyone and everything around us appears out of control?

God invites us to be free from fear of others' lack of obedience or trustworthiness. God never blamed Moses for the Israelites' behavior. Their choices angered God, but Moses remained God's friend. God did not deem the moral failure of the Israelites a reflection of Moses' inadequacy as their leader. And friend, your family member's moral failure is not a reflection of your inadequacy either. Self-sufficiency suggests our involvement in others' lives determines their outcome, but that's giving humanity way too much credit. Surrender solidifies that each person is in God's hands and answers only to Him with their choices. We may not be the perfect spouse, parent, child, or sibling, but their choices ultimately remain their own.

Sometimes in our inadequacy and shame we anticipate being let down by others because we feel like we deserve to be. We expect to be disappointed because we feel like a giant heap of disappointment. We view ourselves negatively so we expect to be treated negatively. We strive to never let anyone else down or we self-sabotage, choosing relationships with people who will most likely wound us.

When others betray us and bring devastation to our lives, we need to remember that God is near to us (e.g., see Psalms 34:18; 46:1; 139:7). God will never let us down. He will always be enough. The more we develop a deep friendship with God, bringing Him our deep hurts, longings, and doubts, the more we will grow to trust Him. And we will also learn to trust our loved ones to His care.

Melissa faced a mountainous mess to climb and started to go to counseling to deal with her grief and anger. She needed to regain some normalcy, but also wanted to know why God had allowed all this to happen to her family. The counselor's assignment left her reeling. "I want you to pray for Jim every day. And for Tina." What?! Melissa frequently prayed for Jim's heart to be changed and for him to become remorseful over his affair. But Tina? She could not even say her name aloud, let alone pray for her. The counselor insisted. "This is more for you than it is for them, Melissa. Trust me in this."

> SURRENDER SOLIDIFIES THAT EACH PERSON IS IN GOD'S HANDS AND ANSWERS ONLY TO HIM WITH THEIR CHOICES.

It took a long time, but eventually trust between Melissa and Jim was restored. Melissa could have allowed her fear of inadequacy to overwhelm her, believing the lies that she deserved to be betrayed. She knew the healing had begun when she agreed to pray for her husband even in the depths of her despair and to intercede for Tina in the midst of her burning anger. It had all started with surrender.

Our fear of inadequacy tells us people will reject, disappoint, or betray us because we deserve it. Or that others' failure is somehow our fault. Our God disagrees. He demands that wrong be made right. He teaches us to turn to Him in our despair and devastation. He asks us to surrender them over to Him, letting Him be God, instead of striving to secure the outcome we want.

# *Intentional Trekking*

## Bible Reading Plan:
Exodus 32:1–24

## Truths for the Journey

- When people betray us, we must make a choice. Will pride seep in taking us beyond justifiable anger to utter vengeance, or will we humbly run to God for help in this devastation?

- Moses turned to God and interceded for those who had betrayed him.

- In our conquest to defeat our fear of inadequacy we can become tempted toward self-sufficiency.

- Our deep fear of inadequacy, of not being enough, will tempt us to believe that they failed us because we weren't good enough to deserve loyalty, honesty, or love.

- When others betray us and bring devastation to our lives, God becomes angered over it.

- God wants us to turn to Him with our disappointments.

## Processing the Journey

1. How important do you believe honesty is in a relationship?

2. Have you ever been lied to? How did that make you feel?

3. Have you ever considered that when others lie, disappoint, or betray you, God Himself becomes angered over your pain?

4. Have you ever allowed a fear of inadequacy to drive you toward self-sufficiency, striving to repair a broken relationship in your own strength and scheming? Why is surrender actually more powerful?

5. Has someone ever treated you poorly and you felt like you deserved it? What does God's reaction toward Aaron's betrayal teach us?

6. Is there someone in your life for whom you need to intercede even though you don't want to do so? Why do you think God taught Moses to intercede for those who had hurt him?

## Passionate Prayer

*Dear Jesus, help me turn to You in my disappointments.
Silence the lies in my mind and heart that suggest I deserve to be
betrayed or disappointed. Show me where I am striving to
control my relationships and how to surrender. Help me
faithfully pray for those who have hurt me, trusting You to be
enough to give me wisdom in those painful relationships.*

## CHAPTER FOURTEEN

# When the Worst Happens

*Moses said, "Please show me your glory."*

*Exodus 33:18*

Wild-child-turned-Jesus-lover Jake quickly swept Cindy off her feet. With his life taking a one-hundred-eighty-degree turn after salvation, Jake ran like a track star toward the Lord. He was sold out for Christ and soon went into ministry.

Cindy kept pace right alongside him, and they found themselves living in a challenging urban area, planting a church. Two years into their marriage, they welcomed newborn Ellie, but soon after, their primary financial supporter pulled out. The fledging church plant closed. Feeling abandoned by God and others, Jake became so disillusioned he left ministry altogether.

Ever creative and energetic, he landed a job at a design studio and poured himself into his new position with his signature vigor. But his heart was straying from God. Deadlines for mockups and proofs came fast and furious, and Jake and the team often pulled all-nighters to prepare for client presentations. Once contracts were signed, the team would go out to celebrate, needing to let off steam, and the drink flowed freely.

Jake came back later and later from these celebrations. Sometimes a coworker drove him home and once or twice he couldn't make it up the front steps without help. Cindy wondered if Jake was returning to old ways, generational habits that had been part of his family growing up, but didn't want to add to his stress to provide for the family by questioning him about it. But then she found liquor hidden in the trunk of his car.

Cindy contacted a pastor friend for advice. She didn't want to betray Jake's trust but she grew increasingly concerned. Also, she was pregnant again. This pastor reached out to Jake and invited him to quit his job and take a less-stressful staff position with the church. He thought removing Jake from the high-charged work environment would get him back on track with his life. Jake agreed, and within a few months seemed to be back to his happy self. He enjoyed playing with Ellie and newborn Ben.

But after a time, Cindy noticed that Jake was falling asleep earlier and earlier in the evenings, and she couldn't put it all down to disrupted sleep patterns with a new baby in the house. He also had a harder time waking up in the morning. One night when she was up with Ben, she noticed Jake's workbag on the kitchen counter. When she moved it to the table she heard a clank. Inside, she found an empty flask. Jake was drinking again, apparently a lot, and while on staff with the church.

Cindy hesitated to talk with the pastor. What if the church dismissed Jake? She remembered how abandoned they had both felt a few years before after the unfortunate experience with the church plant. Would he have another crisis of faith? She also worried how they would make it if he lost his job. How could she go back to work with a toddler and new baby? What about insurance? Would God take care of them? Her worst fears threatened to smother her.

Maybe your worst fear isn't reflected in a flask, but when you behold your own reflection of circumstances you shudder all the same. Maybe it's a frightening diagnosis. Maybe a pile of bills you don't know how you'll pay. A child you have not spoken to in months and you don't even know where they are or you know exactly where they currently lie in a hospital bed and you doubt they'll ever come back home. Maybe it's that nagging feeling that something has gone wrong in your marriage and your worst fear of abandonment looms large. Maybe it's a computer screen that won't leave you alone in the wee hours of the night while you struggle to remain faithful. Our enemy taunts us with these fears, with larger-than-life problems that we cannot wish away. How can God be good in the midst of them?

Moses' worst fear comes true in Exodus 33. God suggests He may abandon His people. After Aaron constructed the golden calf and the people engaged in revelry and worshiped it, the Lord's anger burned intensely. Instead of personally going with them into the promised land, He would send an angel to guide and protect them to ensure His wrath would not break out against them, destroying them on the way. When the people of Israel heard this, they mourned greatly. Moses, however, completely freaks out.

Moses already begged God to "blot me out of your book that you have written" (Ex. 32:32) if He would not forgive them for the golden calf incident. In case you don't speak ancient Hebrew, that's the equivalent of "Just take my life. I'd rather die." Moses is at his breaking point. He simply cannot take one more step without God's assurance. He told Him,

> "If your presence will not go with me, *do not bring us up from here.* For how shall it be known that I have found favor in your sight, I and your people? Is it not in your going with us, so that we are distinct, I and your people, from every other people on the face of the earth?"—Exodus 33:15–16

Moses is at his wit's end knowing that if God ceases leading, Moses will surely be inadequate on his own and the entire deliverance operation will fail. He cries out to God for answers, begging Him to stay.

In this discourse we can see several aspects of God's character of which Moses is confident: He is powerful and purposeful. He subdues His enemies. He has given Moses His favor. But there are some things of which Moses remains unsure. Can God be trusted not to abandon him? Moses knows God holds the power to *make good* on His promises to bring the people into the promised land, but he struggles to trust that God will *be good* on their behalf. He knows what God can do, but he needs assurance of what God is like. Moses begs Him, "Please show me your glory" (Ex. 33:18).

God's glory is simply the essence of His character. Oh, the tenderness of God in this moment! He could have answered Moses simply and in straightforward facts: *I am* LORD. *I am good, and merciful and gracious. I brought you out of Egypt. I destroyed your enemies before you. I fed you in the wilderness. I miraculously provided water.*

> "THERE IS NO PART OF ME BUT GOODNESS. I CREATED YOU TO SHOW YOU ALL OF MY GOODNESS. I WILL NEVER LEAVE YOU OR FORSAKE YOU." MOSES NEEDED TO KNOW THERE WAS ONE WHO WOULD NEVER LIE OR LEAVE.

But He offers Moses so much more. "I will make *all my goodness* pass before you and will proclaim before you my name 'The LORD'" (Ex. 33:19a). Let's just pause right there for a moment and feebly try to imagine that. All God's goodness passing before us at once. All. Of. It. I can't even.

And God reminds Moses of His Name: Yahweh. The LORD. The God who creates, the God who enters relationship. To hear the very voice of God speaking His divine essence and purpose. Pardon me while I shake off the shivers. *Moses, I created you to be in relationship with Me. There is no part of Me but goodness. I created you to show you all of My goodness. I will never leave you or forsake you.*

In many ways this demonstrates a tremendous breakthrough moment for Moses. He has given up the lie that he needs to be the one who is adequate enough to bring the people into the promised land. It's not about him reaching a certain height in leadership and being good enough. He still needed to understand the depths of God's character. Could he really trust the goodness of this God in whom he had placed all of his hope?

How about you and me? Can we confidently say as David did, "I believe that I shall look upon the goodness of the LORD in the land of the living"? (Ps. 27:13). Are we certain of God's goodness? Or do we struggle to believe His promises to never abandon us and to always be good on our behalf? Unlike Moses, we have God's Word to daily display His goodness to His people throughout decades and even millennia.

But I love how in Moses' deepest desperation, God did not just proclaim His goodness and tell Moses to take His word for it. God in His great mercy *displayed His goodness* right before Moses' weary eyes. He tucked Moses away and tenderly covered his eyes, washing all of His goodness over Moses' dry and brittle heart, removing His touch only to allow Moses to see His majesty. I find this reassurance from God to Moses so beautiful in the wake of Aaron's deep betrayal. Surely Moses needed to know there was One who would never lie or leave. There was nothing left for Moses to do. No striving or conniving. Just surrender. He needed only for God to arrive and reveal His goodness to him.

When our worst fear comes true, we often cannot see how to move forward, and we may even wish for death. We too beg God to show us His goodness. Maybe it will come in the kindness of a friend. Maybe it will be a fresh wind of God's grace and mercy giving us strength to go on in the middle of "whys." A time out in a quiet place where we experience God's tender touch. Or in revisiting an old familiar Bible story that reminds us of our God who topples giants and tames lions.

For Cindy it came in the mail. A newsletter arrived from a good friend, a man who had mentored Jake right after he accepted Christ. He was on the board of a rehab center in the next state that could help Jake. Cindy fervently prayed for her husband to be willing to go. She left the newsletter where Jake would see it. She begged God for this to be the miracle in Jake's life.

Jake agreed to try. He felt time with his former mentor as well as rehab might be what he needed for a lasting breakthrough. His current church agreed to give him a leave of absence, and Jake kissed his family goodbye. He would fly out, spend the night in a hotel near the airport, and be picked up the next morning by his mentor and driven to the rehab center where he would begin his recovery.

Except Jake never woke up. Jake died that night in his sleep from alcohol poisoning, leaving Cindy a young widow with two small children. Cindy felt abandoned. By Jake. And by God. She moved in with her parents and struggled for several months with how to move forward.

Cindy did not get the ideal ending you and I wanted to read. But if you met Cindy today, you'd see the perspective she holds now about that trying season. She recounts Jake's deep desire to break the chains of addiction, abuse, and poverty that had been part of his family's story for generations. He so desperately wanted his children to know a better life, but his addictions continually chased him. Cindy explains, "For the chains of addiction to be broken in Jake's family, I believe Jake needed to be broken himself. God watched Jake battle long enough and He took Him home to victory. And I don't ever worry that my children will follow in their dad's footsteps, knowing what they do about his life."

> OUR GOD HAS PROMISED TO NEVER LEAVE US OR FORSAKE US. WE NEVER NEED TO FEAR HIS ABANDONMENT.

Our God has promised to never leave us or forsake us. We never need to fear His abandonment. He is the same God who is walking with you and me today—all the way to victory. Even in the dark hours of midnight stumbling through life as our worst fear flashes us in the face.

Jesus shared a parable with His disciples about a need at midnight. A man discovered he would soon have a guest arriving in the middle of the night. With nothing to serve, the man panicked. Failing to offer a meal no matter the hour of arrival amounted to ultimate shame—toward the guest, on the host, and the village at large for failing to offer proper hospitality. The host runs next door to his neighbor, pounding on the door in the wee hours of the night.

> PRAYER OFFERS AN INVITATION FOR DIVINE INTERVENTION AND GOD WILL ALWAYS RSVP.

Jesus presents a plot twist. The shameful neighbor does the unthinkable. He denies him. Sends him home empty-handed with no regard for his plight. Jesus' audience assuredly gasped over such selfish behavior. As Americans we balk at the host's audacity, while Jesus' audience would have shuddered in shame over the neighbor's utter disregard for social expectations. The entire village would be shamed for this, not just the individual.

Jesus' point? Of course, a neighbor would answer the door! Of course, the neighbor would aid in offering hospitality! And what is the context in Jesus teaching this parable? Prayer. The disciples asked Jesus about prayer. How they ought to pray. And while Jesus modeled the Lord's prayer for them after their request, He followed it up with this story. He wanted them to grasp the heart of the One whom they supplicated. Prayer offers an invitation for divine intervention and God will always RSVP. He would never turn them away in their moment of desperation. Even at midnight.

Jesus followed this story with stunning questions.

> "What father among you, if his son asks for a fish, will instead of a fish give him a serpent; or if he asks for an egg, will give him a scorpion? If you then, who are evil, know how to give good gifts to your children, how much more will the heavenly Father give the Holy Spirit to those who ask him!"—Luke 11:11–13

The Holy Spirit. The Comforter. The Guide. The Helper. The One who shines light upon our shuddering circumstances, providing wisdom and strength to help us in our time of need. Cindy felt entirely alone. Moses felt alone. When our worst fear unfolds, we feel alone. But we will never walk alone. Not one single step. In the dead of night when the darkness envelops, threatening to steal from within us our very last breath, even then the light of Christ illumines us. The hand of God cradles us. The goodness of God passes in front of us like a gentle breeze bringing breath back into our lungs. And maybe in that moment, all we can do is breathe and wait for Jesus' arrival. But He will always open the door of His perfect provision and provide what we need.

# Intentional Trekking

## Bible Reading Plan:
Exodus 32:30–33:23

## Truths for the Journey

- Sometimes we know what God can do, but we need assurance of what God is like.

- God created you to show you all of His goodness.

- Jesus will never abandon us.

- The human heart desperately needs to know we have One who will never lie or leave.

- Jesus did not just teach us how to pray, He introduced us to the heart of the Father to whom we pray.

- Prayer offers an invitation for divine intervention and God will always RSVP.

## Processing the Journey

1. What is the worst fear you have ever had to face? How did Jesus meet you in that fear?

2. Have you ever felt abandoned by God? What did you do in that moment?

3. How have you experienced the goodness of God in your life?

4. Has your perspective over that fear changed over time? How so?

5. How does the gift of the Holy Spirit bring comfort to you?

## Passionate Prayer

*Dear Jesus, forgive me when I forget Your goodness. Help me remember that You will never leave or lie. You will always give me what I need to get through whatever life throws my way. Remind me of the Holy Spirit living inside of me, giving me strength, power, and peace in any and every circumstance.*

CHAPTER **FIFTEEN**

# Disobedience and Delays

*Then the LORD said, "I have pardoned, according to your word.*
*But truly, as I live, and as all the earth shall be filled with*
*the glory of the LORD, none of the men who have seen my glory*
*and my signs that I did in Egypt and in the wilderness, and yet*
*have put me to the test these ten times and have not obeyed my*
*voice, shall see the land that I swore to give their fathers.*
*And none of those who despised me shall see it."*

*Numbers 14:20–23*

Kayla effused energy. Her eyes sparkled when she smiled and you could not resist smiling back at the sight of her wide grin and giggle. She and her daughter Olivia lived in our neighborhood and our paths crossed often. She was a woman who loved to help others—with anything. Then Kayla received shocking news—a diagnosis of a debilitating disease that would drastically change her life. Around that time a mutual acquaintance invited her to her first ever Bible study, where they were reading through *The Purpose Driven*

*Life.* She devoured Scripture while her body began to deteriorate.

One morning at home, Kayla stumbled upon a televangelist who suggested her illness came from a lack of faith. God did not want her body to stop functioning properly, the preacher claimed, and if she simply asked God to heal her, He most certainly would. Kayla began to pray. Her legs were weakening significantly as her condition advanced, so she decided she needed to start bike riding. She found a red ten-speed at a garage sale, and when she told the owner of the bike her testimony, the woman insisted she take the bike free of charge. Kayla accepted this to be a sign from God that as she peddled in faith, He would provide her healing.

With the same energy she always had, she boldly told everyone God's plan to heal her. She rode that red ten-speed everywhere. But then her balance began to slip and she fell several times. Her disease progressed. Kayla grew disillusioned. She peddled, God provided. That was the plan. But her limbs lacked strength and her heart slipped into despair.

After several months of her disease continuing to worsen, the unthinkable happened. Kayla took her own life, leaving behind a husband and two daughters. She wrote them a letter stating that she no longer wished to burden them with her disease. Over and over her grieving husband kept saying, "She should have let us decide that. She needs to be here."

The guilt and grief relentlessly assailed young Olivia's shattered heart. Could *she* have prevented this from happening? Could *she* have convinced her mom that she was not a burden to her?

I arrived at the funeral and sat down stiffly. The room was packed, though nobody wanted to be there. None of us should have been there. But we were. Hearts broken and minds reeling. Things like this don't happen to people we know. This is the stuff of talk shows and news stories, not our small-town community. Why would Kayla think that ending her life so suddenly and unexpectedly would actually be a gift to her family? None of this made sense.

People tried to offer explanations. "Well, you never know what goes on behind closed doors," or other strange sayings that presumably are supposed to offer some sort of guarantee that this horror will never cross their own front porch. There had to be a secret the family wasn't telling. But no amount of speculation will ever release the suffocating feeling of a family's broken heart. Why would the details matter anyway? She was gone and not a single one of the hundreds of people crowded into that worship center could bring her back.

Olivia hated herself. She retraced countless conversations and interactions between her and her mom, barraging her brain with blame over why she had not seen the signs. She withdrew. She felt like her little sister was without their mom because she herself had not protected her from this tragedy. She descended into the darkest of pits where no one could reach her and she could not see the light above her head. And Kayla, who had unexpectedly taken her own life, could never have imagined that she would also change forever the lives of the others in her family when she chose to end her own.

> WE WONDER. *IF I HAD BEEN WISER, KINDER, MORE CAPABLE, OR STRONGER, COULD I HAVE CHANGED THE OUTCOME SOMEHOW?*

How do you explain to a child the unfairness of it all? How do you teach her that an invisible God is enough when her visible world has been shattered? In our humanness we want someone to blame. Our pointing finger needs direction. We wonder. *If I had been wiser, kinder, more capable, or stronger, could I have changed the outcome somehow?* When our finger searches for an object to blame and we cannot seem to locate one, we instinctively begin to blame ourselves. That's what happened to Kayla. When she did not experience the healing she so desperately pleaded and peddled to reach, she blamed her faltering faith.

Just like Olivia blamed herself for not stopping her.

While thankfully most of us will not wonder if we should

shoulder the blame for a situation as horrific as Olivia's, we still have two pointer fingers that seem to find their way back to our own aching hearts. Maybe it's a career that never unfolded because you somehow never could get the attention of the right people or be in the right place at the right time. Maybe it's a life of singleness and you wonder why any promises of a potential relationship continue to wither. Maybe it's a prodigal child and you feel that their choices came from your inadequate parenting. Or an unhealthy marriage you never confronted. Maybe it's a financial crisis that came from you passively trusting your spouse to do the right thing and found out they didn't. Maybe it's a dissolved marriage and you wonder what more you could have done to make it work. And that wagging finger taunts you with "what ifs" and "if onlys" tempting you to believe you should take all the blame.

After two years of wandering in the wilderness, constructing the tabernacle, and experiencing God's faithful provision of water and manna, the time has come for the Israelites to cross over into the promised land. So Moses gathers twelve leaders, one from each tribe, and sends them into the land as spies to report back to the people. For forty days the spies scout out Canaan from north to south and bring back samplings of a rich, fertile land.

However, the spies returned with bad news as well as good. The land contained huge, fortified cities. Several enemy nations already occupied the land, and they would need to go to battle to take it from them. The people were aghast at the description of the giants who roamed the land. The spies spread a fearful report, convincing the Israelites that if they crossed over into the land, they would be consumed.

In this moment, the people decide to fire Moses as Desert Director and elect a new leader to take them back to Egypt. "Would that we had died in the land of Egypt! Or would that we had died in this wilderness! Why is the LORD bringing us into this land, to fall by the sword? Our wives and our little ones will become a prey. Would it not be better for us to go back to Egypt?" (Num. 14:2–3). Two of the spies, Joshua and Caleb, plead with the people to abandon this rebellion against God, insisting that God promised them the land and He will surely give it to them. Just when the people try to stone them, God's glory descends in front of the tent of meeting.

And the very thing they suggested would be preferable over entering the promised land? God granted their wish. *You don't want to go on? Fine.*

> Say to them, "As I live, declares the LORD, what you have said in my hearing I will do to you: your dead bodies shall fall in this wilderness, and of all your number, listed in the census from twenty years old and upward, who have grumbled against me, not one shall come into the land where I swore that I would make you dwell, except Caleb the son of Jephunneh, and Joshua the son of Nun. But your little ones, who you said would become a prey, I *will* bring in, and *they* shall know the land that *you* have rejected."—Numbers 14:28–31

Suddenly Moses' assignment as Desert Director became a lifelong endeavor. Why? Because of others' failure to believe God. And all of their children suffered for their faithlessness as well. This is one of the hardest lessons we will face in this life to overcome our fear of failure or inadequacy. When we believe and obey God, but the failure of others to do so results in a long-term consequence, we are relegated to withstand the effects right alongside them. It seems so unfair . . . so unjust on God's part to make Moses continue leading a rabble bent on rebellion and for the children to remain in the wilderness.

I think there are two big lessons for us in this. What do we do when life feels unfair? When we don't get what we feel we deserve? We can become bitter, or better, depending on how we respond. Will we trust God's work in our lives even when it seems like we should be somewhere else doing something else but because of others' failure we are stuck here? Do we blame ourselves, rehearsing the old lies that it's due to our own inadequacy that others made a poor choice?

In the opening verses of 1 Corinthians 10, Paul informs us that the wanderings of the Israelites were written down as warnings for us. In other words, Moses wasn't just relegated to leading this rabble, he was going to lead every Christ follower from the beginning of church history all the way to Jesus' return. Moses' story is for all of us—a call to trust God fully, even and especially when it doesn't make sense and feels harsh.

THE CHILDREN WHO REMAINED IN THE WILDERNESS WITH GOD AMONG THEM GREW TO BE GIANTS THEMSELVES. GIANTS OF FAITH.

The second lesson is this: our obedience to God and trust in His character in this moment results in eternal impact. Others' failures should never drive us to look inside ourselves; they should always point us to look to God for answers and understanding. Only He can give us the vision and perspective to know how to respond. That wagging finger ought to flip over to an open palm ready to hand over our questions regarding the unfairness of it all.

We just may not see or know whom God is calling us to affect in the future. It's a reminder that we don't live for ease in this life, we live for a glory that far outweighs any pleasure this earth can offer. When Moses entered the tent of meeting with God, he witnessed a glory far beyond the beauty of the promised land of Israel. Moses did not need his circumstances to change to receive all the fullness of God. Neither did Israel. God already dwelt among them—they beheld His glory descending among them, signs and wonders of provision and protection. They did not need to go into the promised land to receive more of God.

And God is slowly changing us from glory to glory to be able to witness this glory ourselves. Sometimes it's painful. Sometimes it's scary. But when we get to heaven and see with our own eyes what awaits us, I believe our only regret will be that we treated our Lord with contempt in failing to trust Him more. We will wonder why we insisted our circumstances needed to change in order for God to be enough for us.

Interestingly, these children who remained in the wilderness with God among them grew to be giants themselves. Giants of faith. When God gave them the green light to enter the promised land so many years later, they responded entirely differently than their parents. "All that you have commanded us we will do, and wherever you send us we will go" (Josh.1:16), they vowed. These are the same children who marched around Jericho trusting God to knock down the walls. They did not waste time pointing fingers at their parents' failures; instead, they followed with open hearts and hands to receive all God had for them. God had been enough in the wilderness and He would be enough now in the promised land.

I will never forget my very first writers retreat. It was a small, intimate gathering, just a dozen of us, and I did not even consider myself a writer at this point, yet here I sat working on a book proposal. All I knew at this point? God told me to study the book of Ezekiel and to write down what He taught me from its pages.

The last night of the retreat, our leader, Kathe, implored us to write our biggest fear on a piece of paper and throw it into the fire. She read from Joshua 1:9. "Have I not commanded you? Be strong and courageous. Do not be frightened, and do not be dismayed, for the LORD your God is with you wherever you go." I can see the letters from that red Sharpie and I can visualize the smoldering paper, the smoke rising, and the consumption of the flames. What did I write on that piece of paper? Only one word.

Enough.

That was my biggest fear. Would God be enough when I faced ridicule or rejection? Would God be enough if I failed? Would God make me enough to step up in obedience or would I fall down in fear?

I remember God's answer in my heart as He reminded me of His constant faithfulness. *Was I enough when you left your family and friends and moved across country? Was I enough when you walked through infertility? Was I enough in your adoptions? Was I enough when your daddy battled cancer until I brought him home? Will you trust Me to be enough in this too?*

*I never needed you to be enough, child. I just want you to trust Me. Will you trust Me now?*

Throughout the gospel accounts Jesus warned His followers of the following:

- We will face rejection (John 16:1–4).

- We will experience tragedy that we don't understand or can't explain (Luke 13:1–5).

- There will be times when God will feel far away and we'll forget His promises of His return and redemption (Matt. 25:1–13; Luke 12:42–48).

We should expect these things in this life. They don't signify God's displeasure; rather, they are depictions of the shattered brokenness of this planet. God promised to be with Moses throughout the entire journey until he returned all the way home, and Jesus promised the same to us. God swore to bring the nation of Israel into the promised land and He accomplished it, despite their unbelief and rebellion.

> WE THINK THAT IF OUR CIRCUMSTANCES CHANGE, THEN WE WILL HAVE WHAT WE NEED. WE FORGET THAT WE ALREADY HAVE ALL OF GOD THAT WE WILL EVER NEED.

Sometimes our circumstances seem to keep us stuck. We think that if they change, then we will have what we need. We look around for someone to blame for the way things are. We might even blame God as the Israelites did. Or we blame ourselves. We forget that we already have all of God that we will ever need. In the wilderness or the promised land. His glory surrounds us in any and every circumstance. We don't need life to be perfect to experience His perfection.

Where is your finger wagging? What is your biggest fear?

Throw it into the fire and allow God to envelop that wagging finger in His own almighty hand. He is enough to make you more than enough to survive any circumstance and follow Him wherever He sends you.

# *Intentional Trekking*

**Bible Reading Plan:**
Numbers 13–14

## Truths for the Journey

- When our finger searches for an object to blame and we cannot seem to locate one, we instinctively begin to blame ourselves.

- When we don't get what we feel we deserve, we can become bitter or better based on how we choose to respond.

- Others' failures should never drive us to look inside ourselves— they should always point us to look to God for answers and understanding.

- God doesn't need us to be enough, He desires that we trust Him.

- Disappointments don't signify God's displeasure; rather, they are depictions of the shattered brokenness of this planet.

- God will accomplish His purposes despite our unbelief and rebellion.

- We don't need perfect circumstances to experience His perfection.

## Processing the Journey

1. Is there a circumstance or a broken relationship in your life for which you blame yourself?

2. Have you ever suffered circumstances due to others' poor choices? How might God use this experience to turn you into a giant of faith?

3. Have you ever cried a "would that" out to the Lord as the Israelites did in Numbers 14:2? If God granted your "would that," how would your life look now?

4. Did the Israelites' "would thats" ultimately change the fulfillment of God's promises to bring the people into the promised land? What benefits occurred in the midst of the consequence?

5. Do you struggle to believe that you need perfect circumstances to experience God's perfection? How does reflecting on the fact that the Israelites already had the fullness of God's presence and provision among them in the wilderness bring hope to your own less-than-ideal circumstances?

6. What is your biggest fear? What keeps you from trusting God with it? Will you trust Him with it now?

## Passionate Prayer

*Dear Jesus, sometimes I feel so responsible to secure the best outcome. I strive, trying to make everyone happy and secure. I confess that I cannot make anyone do anything they do not want to do. You alone guide their hearts. Forgive me when I try to manipulate instead of allowing You to manage their lives. Help me let You be God. Help me believe that I have all of You that I will ever need. I don't need perfect circumstances to experience Your perfection. You are with me in the wilderness as well as in the promised land. And You will be enough.*

## CHAPTER SIXTEEN

# God's Ultimate Plan

*Then Moses and Aaron gathered the assembly together*
*before the rock, and he said to them, "Hear now, you rebels:*
*shall **we** bring water for you out of this rock?"*

*Numbers 20:10*

Truth telling moment: I've always hated this story in Scripture. For someone who has battled fear of inadequacy her whole life, it instantly ignites my deepest fear within me. In this one act of disobedience, Moses gets counted out and forfeits entry into the promised land. What?! I thought I served a God of grace! This is a tough one for me. But when I place this snapshot in the overall context of Moses' life, I realized something.

Something significant.

For forty years Moses had interceded for the people of Israel. He had served them and cared for them, instructed them, and led them faithfully through the desert at God's command. But you know who we never read about Moses interceding for? Himself. We're not told in Scripture if Moses ever brought his anger issues before God or confessed to God how afraid he felt. We just do not know if he ever admitted his own sinfulness and struggle with bitterness. From the biblical record we might infer that he talked to God about everyone and everything else.

Do we allow God access into the hidden caverns of our hearts where our real fears and struggles dwell? Or do we divert His attention toward other people and matters that seem more comfortable to discuss?

Sometimes I think talking to God about my own struggles for success or significance seems selfish. It feels counterintuitive to talk to an almighty God about my fear of not feeling successful or others perceiving me as inadequate. After all, He can do anything. I almost wonder at times if He can wrap His omnipotent mind around my insecurity and self-doubt. Can you relate?

What's interesting is that God commands His people, "Do not fear, do not be afraid," more than any other command in Scripture. So why do we withhold our fears from Him when He already knows they're there? Maybe the real lesson in Moses' story is that we need to stop stuffing our fear of failure and inadequacy and bring it out in the open before God once and for all—to finally make peace with Him, releasing the outcome. When we can express our deepest fear, or our worst imagined outcome to God, we invite God to demonstrate His greatest glory, goodness, mercy, and compassion (Ex. 33:12–23).

Moses spent countless hours in God's presence in the tent of meeting. He interceded for the people of Israel incessantly. God outlined for Moses His heart and plans to dwell among the people, yet Moses never felt comfortable bringing his own struggles, dreams, and longings. He continued to fear God's rejection. Psalm 90 gives great insight into how Moses viewed God in general and his life of service to Him. Unlike the Pentateuch, which provides snapshots of Moses' dialogue with God during specific instances, this psalm paints a broad brushstroke across the canvas of Moses' heart.

Lord, you have been our dwelling place
    in all generations.
Before the mountains were brought forth,
    or ever you had formed the earth and the world,
    from everlasting to everlasting you are God.

You return man to dust
    and say, "Return, O children of man!"
For a thousand years in your sight
    are but as yesterday when it is past,
    or as a watch in the night.

You sweep them away as with a flood; they are like a dream,
    Like grass that is renewed in the morning:
In the morning it flourishes and is renewed;
    in the evening it fades and withers.

For we are brought to an end by your anger;
    by your wrath we are dismayed.
You have set our iniquities before you,
    our secret sins in the light of your presence.

For all our days pass away under your wrath;
    we bring our years to an end like a sigh.
The years of our life are seventy,
    or even by reason of strength eighty;
yet their span is but toil and trouble;
    they are soon gone, and we fly away.
Who considers the power of your anger,
    and your wrath according to the fear of you?

So teach us to number our days
    that we may get a heart of wisdom.

Return, O LORD! How long?
　Have pity on your servants!
Satisfy us in the morning with your steadfast love,
　that we may rejoice and be glad all our days.
Make us glad for as many days as you have afflicted us,
　and for as many years as we have seen evil.
Let your work be shown to your servants,
　and your glorious power to their children.
Let the favor of the Lord our God be upon us,
　and establish the work of our hands upon us;
　yes, establish the work of our hands!

As far as we know, this is the only psalm written by Moses. How would you describe Moses' general sentiment? Does this sound like a man curling up in a loving father's lap? Or a weary man uncertain what his Deity may do on his behalf? Moses still appears to wrestle with the certainty of God's goodness in his life, citing God's anger and affliction with greater frequency than either His love, kindness, or tenderness. Scholars don't necessarily agree at what point in his life Moses penned this psalm. Scripture, however, does remind us that Moses was a man of great humility—the most humble man in all the earth (Num. 12:3). Moses readily acknowledged God's tremendous power and miraculous works. He viewed himself infinitely less capable than this great and glorious God whom he served. Unlike his first encounter with God back in Exodus 3, when Moses insists he is not very familiar with Yahweh or with His power or capability, this psalm expresses Moses' understanding of how vast and powerful God is!

Contrast Moses' description of God in Psalm 90 with the repeated description of Himself that God commands Moses to teach the people through Aaron. God desired this blessing to be spoken over the people of Israel continually—it would become second nature to His people because they would hear it so many times.

The LORD spoke to Moses, saying, "Speak to Aaron and his sons, saying, Thus you shall bless the people of Israel: you shall say to them,

> The LORD bless you and keep you;
> the LORD make his face to shine upon you and be gracious to you;
> the LORD lift up his countenance upon you and give you peace.

"So shall they put my name upon the people of Israel, and I will bless them."—Numbers 6:22–27

God desired that the people know He longed to bless, to keep, to bring His light, to extend grace, to offer peace . . . to call them His own. That sounds much different to me than Moses' description of God in Psalm 90. God paints a polar opposite picture of Himself in this blessing He commanded to be spoken over His people until it rolled off the tongue in familiarity. The beauty and majesty of God is that both descriptions of God in these scriptural passages are equally true. God needs to be revered as altogether other and separate from humanity in His holiness, while at the same time, present and close in His kindness and care. In our finite mentality we often end up leaning toward one view or the other about God and fail to grasp the entirety of His greatness and goodness at the same time. Or we assign one aspect of God to a circumstance in which we want Him to be powerful, while asking Him to be tender and kind in moments of rebellion or distrust of His plans. While Moses easily accepted the greatness of God's capabilities, it seems he may still have difficulty fully grasping the kindness of His character.

When we lived in North Carolina, our town held an annual Christmas Parade down Main Street. You needed to park a few blocks away and walk until you found an open spot along the curb. I loaded Eliana and Nathan into the double stroller and set out to find a good place to wait for the parade to begin. People poured into the half-mile-long downtown. Nearly everyone in our small town came to watch.

About ten minutes into the parade, wet sloshy snow began to fall. I grabbed the kids, stuffed them back into the stroller, and attempted to shield them with our waterproof picnic blanket. Eliana, not even three years old, wailed, and Nathan kicked his chubby little not-yet-walking legs violently, kicking his sister. Time for plan B.

> IN THE MIDST OF THE STORMS OF LIFE, GOD LONGS TO KEEP US. HE INVITES US TO NESTLE DEEP WITH HIMSELF, KEEPING US DRY AND WARM, WHILE THE STORM PASSES BY.

We were hemmed in on every side, and trying to roll the kids back to the car in a double side-by-side stroller proved impossible. I extracted them from their seats, stuck one on each hip, and wrapped the blanket around us, trying to study the sky for any signs of the snow stopping. Eliana squeezed her little legs and arms around me so tightly I thought I might snap in two. She buried her face in my neck and I felt her hot tears trickle down. She could not get close enough to me in her fear and discomfort. If she could melt and ooze inside of me I think she would have done so.

Nathan, on the other hand, found the blanket stifling and the snow exciting. (And who says boys and girls aren't different!) He thrashed about, trying to get the blanket obstructing his vision off of his head. He didn't want to miss one second of the parade regardless. He wriggled his chubby little legs, trying to slip himself out of my grasp. He did not want my protection. He despised caution! He'd bear the wet snow just to enjoy the parade. He held no thought of getting sick, not being able to see way down on the ground with everyone's blankets huddled about them, nor the parade itself stopping momentarily anyway!

In the midst of the storms of life, God longs to keep us. He invites us to nestle deep within Himself, keeping us dry and warm, while the storm passes by. We don't need to study the sky; God already knows what we can bear. We won't miss any celebrations tucked safely in His arms. But will we trust Him? Will we press in and allow Him to keep us or will we squirm to wriggle free, afraid we are missing out on something grand and exciting because God has momentarily shielded our vision, allowing us only to see His strong arms around us?

Moses struggled to believe the certainty of God's goodness and in the middle of a perfect storm, he pushed away from God, deciding to take matters into his own hands. Moses had held the role of Desert Director for nearly forty years now. Not much changed over this span of time. The last time the Israelites stood in this place was thirty-eight years ago, right after the spies returned from the land. As soon as trouble struck, the people complained and blamed Moses. Read through Numbers 20:1–10 below. A lot is going on:

> And the people of Israel, the whole congregation, came into the wilderness of Zin in the first month, and the people stayed in Kadesh. And Miriam died there and was buried there.
>
> Now there was no water for the congregation. And they assembled themselves together against Moses and against Aaron. And the people quarreled with Moses and said, "Would that we had perished when our brothers perished before the LORD! Why have you brought the assembly of the LORD into this wilderness, that we should die here, both we and our cattle? And why have you made us come up out of Egypt to bring us to this evil place? It is no place for grain or figs or vines or pomegranates, and there is no water to drink." Then Moses and Aaron went from the presence of the assembly to the entrance of the tent of meeting and fell on their faces. And the glory of the LORD appeared to them, and the LORD spoke to Moses, saying, "Take the staff, and assemble the congregation, you and Aaron your brother, and *tell the rock* before their eyes to

yield its water. *So you shall bring water out of the rock for them and give drink to the congregation and their cattle.*" And Moses took the staff from before the LORD, as he commanded him.

Now if you read through that quickly, you may not notice anything drastically wrong with God's words, but for Moses, this very conversation included God's warnings. As soon as God spoke thus to Moses, alarm sirens should have sounded throughout the camp. *God suggested Moses was the one bringing the water out of the rock.* The last time God suggested to Moses that he had been the one who had led the people out of Egypt, Moses resolutely disagreed with God. Look at God's words:

> And the LORD said to Moses, "Go down, for your people, whom you brought up out of the land of Egypt, have corrupted themselves. They have turned aside quickly out of the way that I commanded them."—Exodus 32:7–8

Look at Moses' humility before the Lord: "But Moses implored the LORD his God and said, 'O LORD, why does your wrath burn hot against your people, whom *you have brought out of the land of Egypt* with great power and with a mighty hand?'" (v. 11).

Moses insists God held the title of Deliverer. Moses merely followed instructions. But in this scenario, Moses accepts God's designation as the miracle worker. In fact, Moses reverts to utter self-reliance. Look at God's directions to Moses the first time the Israelites faced a beverage crisis:

> And the LORD said to Moses, "Pass on before the people, taking with you some of the elders of Israel, and take in your hand the staff with which you struck the Nile, and go. Behold, I will stand before you there on the rock at Horeb, *and you shall strike the rock,* and water shall come out of it, and the people will drink."—Exodus 17:5–6

Moses remembered God's previous directions from over three dozen years earlier, ran with them, and ceased listening to God carefully. Maybe his bitterness blocked his ability to hear God.

Look at how Moses speaks to the people this go-around:

> Then Moses and Aaron gathered the assembly together before the rock, and he said to them, *"Hear now, you rebels: shall we bring water for you out of this rock?"* And Moses lifted up his hand and struck the rock with his staff twice, and water came out abundantly, and the congregation drank, and their livestock.—Numbers 20:10–11

Moses responds angrily to the people, implying they hold responsibility for his bitterness due to their rebellion. He assumes responsibility for their care and resorts to name-calling in his frustration. He leaves God entirely out of the equation. As a result, God refused to allow Moses entrance into the land of promise, the land he promised to Abraham, Isaac, Jacob, and their descendants.

But this isn't the end of Moses' story. Even in his failure to relinquish his fears and fully trust God, he still makes it into the promised land, the everlasting land promised to each of us. In fact, he was the first to witness Jesus, the Prophet Who Was to Come, and of whom God promised the people through Moses, revealed in all of His glory, standing on the mountain during the transfiguration. Moses and Elijah, along with Peter, James, and John. The only humans to behold the glory to be revealed at the end of the ages (see Deut. 18; Luke 9:28–31).

MOSES WAS ONE OF THE FIRST TO BE SHOWN THAT THE *LAND* HAD NEVER BEEN THE PLACE OF PROMISE. RATHER, THE PROMISE WAS GOD HIMSELF.

Moses was one of the first to be shown that the *land* had never been the place of promise. Rather, the promise was God Himself. Dwelling in their midst. Conquering sin and death. All of God with all of them. Unveiled. Forever. And while we may fight against our flaws, wrestle with our fears, stuff our struggles, and wonder why we still feel stuck, our great God of mercy will still make good on His promises and lead us all the way home. This is grace.

Moses sat with the Lord face to face. He experienced communion with God unlike any other human on the face of the earth. God's Spirit rested upon him. Moses spent forty years of his life interceding for the people of Israel. We read of him asking for wisdom to lead, for pardon for the Israelites and for his own family members who betrayed him. He asked for guidance and victory in battle, for favor, but he still reverted back to a moment of striving to bring water from the rock and silence the rejection and abandonment of his fellow Israelites. Moses decided that Yahweh, the God of relationship—the One who vowed to never leave or lie and who would continually provide for His people, was not enough in this moment. Moses seems to view himself simply as a servant, rather than a beloved son.

Where in my own heart am I tempted to continue striving because I wish to avoid confrontation, be spared from rejection, or fear abandonment? Do I view myself as a beloved daughter able to come crawl in my Daddy's lap and share my heart with Him? While at the same time remember He is an unimaginably vast, omniscient, holy, and powerful God? Which aspect of God do I have a harder time keeping in perspective—or believing He will be enough?

As I pore through my own times before the Lord, I realize that I bring my husband, my children, friends, and extended family to Him. I pray for those with whom I share the gospel or the Word. I pray for my church and my community. But how often do I bring my own junk—my own fear of inadequacy—before Him for healing? How often do I cry out for spiritual victory and success in the lives of others while holding onto areas of my own life that need His transforming power? Why do I try and hide these inadequacies from the very One who knows exactly where they are hidden within the caverns of my heart?

God wanted Moses to come to Him as His child and lay his struggles at His feet. His personal struggles. His heartaches. His fears. All the things he hated about himself. God wanted Moses to come not as Moses the mighty leader, nor the chosen intercessor, but as His child. He wanted to be Moses' father and friend. God wanted to fulfill Moses' deepest desire for belonging and identity. Moses did not need to fit in with the Egyptian royal court. He did not need to be respected or accepted by the people of Israel. He did not need to be successful in his current role to earn God's favor. He needed to allow God full access to his heart.

And so do we.

Let's not spend years communing with God, learning and communicating His laws, witnessing Him work, and serving Him tirelessly, only to fail to give Him that last sliver of our hearts He longs to transform.

What are you keeping from the God who longs to keep you? What keeps you striving, wriggling to be free so you don't miss a thing, instead of nestling in surrender into your Father's loving arms?

Is it fear of inadequacy?

Is it fear of shame if your children don't turn out successfully?

Is it fear of humiliation if your marriage falls apart?

Is it fear of failure to achieve the title, position, role, dollar amount, size, or success?

Is it fear of feeling insignificant if you don't find that calling out there that feels Instagram worthy?

Is it being alone?

Have you brought it before the Lord for healing? Will you bring it to Him now?

When we surrender that fear to our Father, we will finally be free. Don't you know that as Moses stood on that mountain, witnessing the glorified Christ, he realized how needlessly he had shouldered the burden of the people of Israel? And how vastly He had misunderstood the kindness and goodness of God?

Jesus stands before you today, friend, in all of His brilliance. He invites you to surrender. He has everything under control. He will make good on every one of His promises and be good on your behalf. He offers Godfidence.

Let's rest in His care.

# Intentional Trekking

## Bible Reading Plan:
Numbers 20; 6:24–26

## Truths for the Journey

- When we can express our deepest fear or our worst imagined outcome to God, we invite God to demonstrate His greatest glory, goodness, mercy, and compassion.

- God desired the people know He longed to bless, to keep, to bring His light, to extend grace, to call them His own.

- What keeps you from the God who longs to keep you?

- When we surrender our fear to our Father, we will finally be free.

- Yahweh—the God of relationship—sought to pierce through Moses' heart allowing him to see himself as more than a servant, but rather a beloved son.

## Processing the Journey

1. How might bitterness prevent us from hearing God?

2. When things go awry and your emotions get the best of you, whom do you most often find yourself blaming? Why do we default into self-sufficiency in those moments instead of turning to our Father for directions?

3. Imagine sitting across from Jesus with your hands in His. What would you whisper to Him? What would you hope to hear Him say?

4. In fearful moments, do you tend to be more like Eliana, pressing in and clinging to God tightly, or Nathan, wriggling free and afraid you might miss something important because your view is obstructed? Can you remember a time you clung tightly to the Lord? What were the circumstances?

5. Can you identify what lies within that sliver of your heart that you tend to keep hidden from God? Do you believe God longs to give you the freedom that surrendering it to Him would bring?

6. When is a time you surrendered a part of your life you had tended to keep hidden? What happened as a result?

## Passionate Prayer

*Dear Jesus, help me rest in Your care. I choose to surrender to what You say knowing that when my heart doesn't feel it, You will be faithful nonetheless. In moments of fear when I revert to striving, bring me back to Your feet, Jesus, so I can surrender once again. Help me desire Your will for me above anything else my heart desires and to trust You will keep me close to You, protecting me and shielding me from any storm I will face in this life. You will be enough.*

# Some Parting Thoughts

When I first brought Eliana home from the hospital, my fear of inadequacy nearly paralyzed me. God and a brave birth mother had courageously entrusted me with this precious life. What in the world were either of them thinking? I would never be enough. As I rocked Eliana in the middle of the night, tears streamed down my face as I begged God to prevent me from messing up as a mom. I wanted to do everything perfectly. There in the quietness of my heart, I felt the Lord whisper, "Child, if she had a perfect mother, why would she need a heavenly Father?" and I realized in that moment I didn't need to be perfect. In fact, every time I messed up as a mom, it would become an opportunity for God to step in and show both of us His grace.

Since that time, I have come face to face with my fear of inadequacy many times. When God meets me in one place of fear, it seems not much time passes until another area of fear reveals itself. It has been a long process, yet God has been faithful. Time and again when I doubted my abilities, questioned God's wisdom in choosing me to be part of what He was doing, or feared I would fail, God reminded me: I am who I am and I AM *Enough*.

# Acknowledgments

To Judy Dunagan and Pam Pugh, the greatest editors I could ever hope to write under! Nothing surfaced my fear of inadequacy like trying to write a book on surrendering my fear of inadequacy—God, in His great grace, entrusted me to your expertise and care! Thank you for taking the ramblings of my heart and racing thoughts in my head and weaving them together into a meaningful message. I would not be the person I am today without you. Nor would this book have ever come into existence.

To the entire team at Moody Publishers—I still pinch myself when I think about the incredible privilege to get to be a tiny part of your incredible team. May the Eternal Word continue to bless the words that you publish for His Name and glory! And grant each and every one of you great joy in this work.

To my family: Jonathan, Eliana, and Nathan—for always offering grace whenever I fall short as a wife and mom. You all are my more-than-enough and true gifts of God to me.

To Kim Erickson, who has been pushing me forward in this journey from day one! I adore you and could not be more grateful for your friendship and for the Lord allowing our paths to cross at DSCC!

To Kathe Wunnenberg, writing coach and encourager extra-ordinaire! God used your Time to Write retreats to change my life forever and I am eternally grateful.

To my Quaranteam, you all helped make this project possible with prayers, encouragement, support, transportation, logistics, and endless hours of listening to me process ideas! I love you all!

To Jesus, who never stops pursuing us, crushing fear, building our faith, and revealing Your kindness and goodness to us. May I run the race marked out for me.

# Notes

1. The term *impostor syndrome* was coined by psychologists Dr. Pauline R. Clance and Dr. Suzanne A. Imes in their 1978 article "The Impostor Phenomenon in High Achieving Women: Dynamics and Therapeutic Intervention," *Psychotherapy: Theory, Research & Practice* 15, no. 3 (1978): 241. They describe a pattern of self-doubt, insecurity, and incompetence often experienced by high achievers despite their success. Dr. Valerie Young built on their findings and calls it "the unconscious belief that—deep down—we're not as bright or capable as others seem to think we are" (quoted in Alex Kekauoha, "Overcoming Impostor Syndrome," Stanford News, November 7, 2019, https://news.stanford.edu/2019/11/07/overcoming-impostor-syndrome/. See Valerie Young, *The Secret Thoughts of Successful Women: Why Capable People Suffer from the Impostor Syndrome and How to Thrive in Spite of It* (New York: Crown Business, 2011).

2. "Identity," Oxford English Dictionary, https://www.lexico.com/en/definition/identity.

3. John D. Hannah, "Exodus," in *The Bible Knowledge Commentary: Old Testament*, John F. Walvoord and Roy B. Zuck, eds. (Colorado Springs: David C. Cook, 1983), 111.

4. Ibid.

5. Matthew Henry, *Matthew Henry's Commentary in One Volume* (Grand Rapids: Zondervan, 1961), 74.

6. John H. Walton, *Ancient Near Eastern Thought and the Old Testament* (Grand Rapids: Baker, 2006), 92.

7. Ibid., 93.

8. Hannah, "Exodus," in *The Bible Knowledge Commentary: Old Testament*, Walvoord and Zuck, eds., 112.

9. Spiro Zodhiates, *The Hebrew–Greek Key Study Bible* (Grand Rapids: Baker Book House, 1984), 1628.

10. Ibid., 1650.

11. "Godfidence," Urban Dictionary, https://www.urbandictionary.com/define.php?term=godfidence.

12. Charles Swindoll, *Moses: A Man of Selfless Dedication* (Nashville: Word Publishing, 1999), 189.

13. Attributed to Winston Churchill.

14. Attributed to D. L. Moody.

15. Francis Brown, Samuel Rolles Driver, and Charles Augustus Briggs, *Enhanced Brown-Driver-Briggs Hebrew and English Lexicon* (Oxford: Clarendon Press, 1977), electronic edition, Logos Bible Software.

The Holy Spirit set the hearts of the early Christians aflame.
What will He do in your heart?

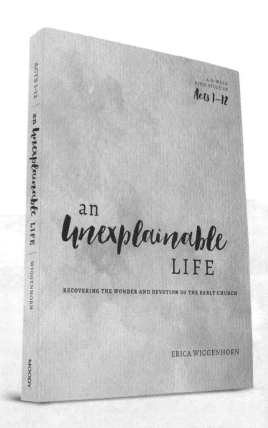

*An Unexplainable Life* is a call to reignite the mission and movement of the early church individually and collectively. This in-depth, 10-week Bible study challenges our modern-day assumptions, inspires us to reclaim the zeal of the apostles, and invites us to join Jesus in His work today.

978-0-8024-1473-1    |    also available as an eBook

# When's the last time you were captivated by Jesus?

Step into the streets of Jerusalem and encounter the Jewish rabbi who turned the world upside down. After rediscovering Jesus in the pages of the book of Luke—or maybe discovering Him for the very first time—you'll see there is no other plan, goal, ambition, or Person worth following but Jesus.

978-0-8024-1909-5 | also available as an eBook

MOODY PUBLISHERS
WOMEN
BIBLE STUDIES

# Will you accept a divine invitation?

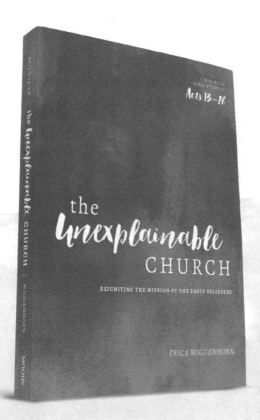

*The Unexplainable Church* is a 10-week inductive study of Acts 13–28 that features scholarly insights, personal reflections, and prompts for application. It will teach by example how to study the Bible deeply, and it will challenge you toward critical life-change: submitting your will to the mission of the church, where life finds its fullest meaning.

978-0-8024-1742-8    |    also available as an eBook

# Discover the secret to a full life.

In this 6-week study of Colossians, Asheritah Ciuciu leads readers to discover the life-altering importance of Jesus' sufficiency and sovereignty. With short meditations for busy days, dig-deep study for days you want more, and supplemental service challenges for leaders, you can study the Bible the way that helps you the most.

978-0-8024-1686-5 | also available as an eBook

MOODY PUBLISHERS
WOMEN
BIBLE STUDIES